Harriet Stowe Beecher

The Salem witchcraft

The planchette mystery and Modern spiritualism

Harriet Stowe Beecher

The Salem witchcraft
The planchette mystery and Modern spiritualism

ISBN/EAN: 9783337375096

Printed in Europe, USA, Canada, Australia, Japan

Cover: Foto ©Lupo / pixelio.de

More available books at **www.hansebooks.com**

HISTORY

OF

SALEM WITCHCRAFT:

A REVIEW

OF

CHARLES W. UPHAM'S GREAT WORK.

FROM THE "EDINBURGH REVIEW."

With Notes,

BY THE EDITOR OF "THE PHRENOLOGICAL JOURNAL."

NEW YORK:
FOWLER & WELLS CO., PUBLISHERS,
753 BROADWAY.
1886.

BIGOTRY. Obstinate or blind attachment to a particular creed; unreasonable zeal or warmth in favor of a party, sect, or opinion; excessive prejudice. The practice or tenet of a bigot.

PREJUDICE. An opinion or decision of mind, formed without due examination of the facts or arguments which are necessary to a just and impartial determination, A previous bent or inclination of mind for or against any person or thing. Injury or wrong of any kind; as to act to the *prejudice* of another.

SUPERSTITION. Excessive exactness or rigor in religious opinions or practice; excess or extravagance in religion; the doing of things not required by God, or abstaining from things not forbidden; or the belief of what is absurd, or belief without evidence. False religion; false worship. Rite or practice proceeding from excess of scruples in religion. Excessive nicety; scrupulous exactness. Belief in the direct agency of superior powers in certain extraordinary or singular events, or in omens and prognostics.—*Webster*.

INTRODUCTION.

The object in reprinting this most interesting review is simply to show the progress made in moral, intellectual, and physical science. The reader will go back with us to a time—not very remote—when nothing was known of Phrenology and Psychology; when men and women were persecuted, and even put to death, through the baldest ignorance and the most pitiable superstition. If we were to go back still farther, to the Holy Wars, we should find cities and nations drenched in human blood through religious bigotry and intolerance. Let us thank God that our lot is cast in a more fortunate age, when the light of revelation, rightly interpreted by the aid of SCIENCE, points to the Source of all knowledge, all truth, all light.

When we know more of Anatomy, Physiology, Physiognomy, and the Natural Sciences generally, there will be a spirit of broader liberality, religious tolerance, and individual freedom. Then all men will hold themselves accountable to God, rather than to popes, priests, or parsons. Our progenitors lived in a time that tried men's souls, as the following lucid review most painfully shows.

S. R. W.

CONTENTS.

	PAGE
The Place	7
The Salemite of Forty Years Ago	8
How the Subject was opened	9
Careful Historiography	10
The Actors in the Tragedy	12
Philosophy of the Delusion	12
Character of the Early Settlement	13
First Causes	15
Death of the Patriarch	16
Growth of Witchcraft	17
Trouble in the Church	18
Rev. Mr. Burroughs	19
Deodat Lawson	20
Parris—a Malignant	20
A Protean Devil	21
State of Physiology	22
William Penn as a Precedent	22
Phenomena of Witchcraft	23
Parris and his Circle	25
The Inquisitions—Sarah Good	26
A Child Witch	27
The Towne Sisters	28
Depositions of Parris and his Tools	31
Goody Nurse's Excommunication	35
Mary Easty	36
Mrs. Cloyse	38
The Proctor Family	40
The Jacobs Family	41
Giles and Martha Corey	42
Decline of the Delusion	44
The Physio-Psychological Causes of the Trouble	45
The Last of Parris	47
"One of the Afflicted"—Her Confession	49
The Transition	50
The Fetish Theory Then and Now	51
The Views of Modern Investigators	53
Importance of the Subject	55

CONTENTS OF THE PLANCHETTE MYSTERY.

	PAGE.
What Planchette is and does (with review of Facts and Phenomena)	63
The Press on Planchette (with further details of Phenomena)	67
Theory First—That the Board is moved by the hands that rest upon it	70
Theory Second—"It is Electricity or Magnetism"	71
Proof that Electricity has nothing to do with it	78
Theory Third—The Devil Theory	79
Theory of a Floating Ambient Mentality	82
"To Daimonion"—The Demon	83
"It is some principle of nature as yet unknown"	85
Theory of the Agency of Departed Spirits	85
PLANCHETTE'S OWN THEORY	89
The Rational Difficulty	92
The Medium—The Doctrine of Spheres	93
The Moral and Religious Difficulty	98
What this Modern Development is, and what is to come of it	102
Conclusion	105
How to work Planchette	106

SPIRITUALISM.

History of Spiritualism	107
Scriptural Views	110
Communion of Saints	113

DR. DODDRIDGE'S DREAM.

Pages 123–125.

SALEM WITCHCRAFT.

THE PLACE.

HE name of the village of Salem is as familiar to Americans as that of any provincial town in England or France is to Englishmen and Frenchmen; yet, when uttered in the hearing of Europeans, it carries us back two or three centuries, and suggests an image, however faint and transient, of the life of the Pilgrim Fathers, who gave that sacred name to the place of their chosen habitation. If we were on the spot to-day, we should see a modern American seaport, with an interest of its own, but by no means a romantic one. At present Salem is suffering its share of the adversity which has fallen upon the shipping trade, while it is still mourning the loss of some of its noblest citizens in the late civil war. No community in the Republic paid its tribute of patriotic sacrifice more generously; and there were doubtless occasions when its citizens remembered the early days of glory, when their fathers helped to chase the retreating British, on the first shedding of blood in the war of Independence. But now they have enough to think of under the pressure of the hour. Their trade is paralyzed under the operation of the tariff; their shipping is rotting in port, except so much of it as is sold to foreigners; there is much poverty in low places and dread of further commercial adversity among the chief citizens, but there is the same vigorous pursuit of intellectual interests and pleasures, throughout the society of the place, that there always is wherever any number of New Englanders have made their homes beside the church, the library, and the school. Whatever other changes may

occur from one age or period to another, the features of natural scenery are, for the most part, unalterable Massachusetts Bay is as it was when the Pilgrims cast their first look over it: its blue waters — as blue as the seas of Greece—rippling up upon the sheeted snow of the sands in winter, or beating against rocks glittering in ice; in autumn the pearly waves flowing in under the thickets of gaudy foliage; and on summer evening the green surface surrounding the amethyst islands, where white foam spouts out of the caves and crevices. On land, there are still the craggy hills, and the jutting promontories of granite, where the barberry grows as the bramble does with us, and room is found for the farmstead between the crags, and for the apple-trees and little slopes of grass, and patches of tillage, where all else looks barren. The boats are out, or ranged on shore, according to the weather, just as they were from the beginning, only in larger numbers; and far away on either hand the coasts and islands, the rocks and hills and rural dwellings, are as of old, save for the shrinking of the forest, and the growth of the cities and villages, whose spires and school-houses are visible here and there.

THE SALEMITE OF FORTY YEARS AGO.

Yet there are changes, marked and memorable, both in Salem and its neighborhood, since the date of thirty-seven years ago. There was then an exclusiveness about the place as evident to strangers, and as dear to natives, as the rivalship between Philadelphia and Baltimore, while far more interesting and honorable in its character. In Salem society there was a singular combination of the precision and scrupulousness of Puritan manners and habits of thought with the pride of a cultivated and traveled community, boasting acquaintance with people of all known faiths, and familiarity with all known ways of living and thinking, while adhering to the customs, and even the prejudices, of their fathers. While relating theological conversations held with liberal Buddhists or lax Mohammedans, your host would whip his horse, to get home at full speed by sunset on a Saturday, that the groom's Sabbath might not be encroached on for five minutes. The houses were hung with odd Chinese copies of English engravings, and furnished with a variety of pretty and useful articles from China, never seen elsewhere, because none but American traders had then achieved any commerce with that country but in tea, nankeen, and silk. The

Salem Museum was the glory of the town, and even of the State. Each speculative merchant who went forth, with or without a cargo (and the trade in ice was then only beginning), in his own ship, with his wife and her babes, was determined to bring home some offering to the Museum, if he should accomplish a membership of that institution by doubling either Cape Horn or the Cape of Good Hope. He picked up an old cargo somewhere and trafficked with it for another; and so he went on—if not rounding the world, seeing no small part of it, and making acquaintance with a dozen eccentric potentates and barbaric chiefs, and sovereigns with widely celebrated names; and, whether the adventurer came home rich or poor, he was sure to have gained much knowledge, and to have become very entertaining in discourse. The houses of the principal merchants were pleasant abodes—each standing alone bèside the street, which was an avenue thick-strewn with leaves in autumn and well shaded in summer. Not far away were the woods, where lumbering went on, for the export of timber to Charleston and New Orleans, and for the furniture manufacture, which was the main industry of the less fertile districts of Massachusetts in those days. Here and there was a little lake—a "pond"—under the shadow of the woods, yielding water-lilies in summer, and ice for exportation in winter—as soon as that happy idea had occurred to some fortunate speculator. On some knoll there was sure to be a school-house. Amid these and many other pleasant objects, and in the very center of the stranger's observations, there was one spectacle that had no beauty in it—just as in the happy course of the life of the Salem community there is one fearful period. That dreary object is the Witches' Hill at Salem; and that fearful chapter of history is the tragedy of the Witch Delusion.

HOW THE SUBJECT WAS OPENED.

Our reason for selecting the date of thirty-seven years ago for our glance at the Salem of the last generation is, that at that time a clergyman resident there fixed the attention of the inhabitants on the history of their forefathers by delivering lectures on Witchcraft. This gentleman was then a young man, of cultivated mind and intellectual tastes, a popular preacher, and esteemed and beloved in private life. In delivering those lectures he had no more idea than his audience that he was entering upon the great work and grand intellectual interest of his life. When he concluded the course, he was unconscious of having offered more than the entertainment of a day; yet the engrossing occupation of seven-and-thirty years for himself, and no little employment and interest for others, have grown out of that early effort. He was requested to print the lectures, and did so. They went through more than one edition; and every time he reverted to the subject, with some fresh knowledge gathered from new sources, he perceived more distinctly how inadequate, and even mistaken, had been his early conceptions of the character of the transactions which constituted the Witch Tragedy. At length he refused to reissue the volume. "I was unwilling," he says in the preface of the book before us, "to issue again what I had discovered to be an insufficient presentation of the subject." Meantime, he was penetrating into mines of materials for history, furnished by the peculiar forms of administration instituted by the early rulers of the province. It was an ordinance of the General Court of Massachusetts, for instance, that testimony should in all cases be taken in the shape of depositions, to be preserved "in perpetual remembrance." In all trials, the evidence of witnesses was taken in writing beforehand, the witnesses being present (except in certain cases) to meet any examination in regard to their recorded testimony. These depositions were carefully preserved, in complete order: and thus we may now know as much about the landed property, the wills, the contracts, the assaults and defamation, the thievery and cheating, and even the personal morals and social demeanor of the citizens of Salem of two centuries and a half ago as we could have done if they had had law-reporters in their courts, and had filed those reports, and preserved the police departments of newspapers like those of the present day. The documents relating to the witchcraft proceedings have been for the most part laid up among the State archives; but a considerable number of them have been dispersed—no doubt from their connection with family history, and under impulses of shame and remorse. Of these, some are safely lodged in literary institutions, and others are in private hands, though too many have been lost.

CAREFUL HISTORIOGRAPHY.

In a long course of years, Mr. Upham, and after him his sons, have searched out all documents they could hear of. When they had reason to believe that any transcription of papers was inaccurate—that gaps had been conjecturally filled up, that dates had been mistaken, or that papers had been transposed, they never rested till they had got hold of the originals, thinking the bad spelling, the rude grammar, and strange dialect of the least cultivated country people less objectionable than the unauthorized amendments of transcribers. Mr. Upham says he has resorted to the originals throughout. Then there were the parish books and church records, to which was committed in early days very much in the life of individuals which would now be considered a matter of private concern, and scarcely fit for comment by next-door neighbors. The primitive local maps and the coast-survey chart, with the markings of original grants to settlers, and of bridges, mills, meeting-houses, private dwellings, forest roads, and farm boundaries, have been preserved. Between these and deeds of conveyance it has been possible to construct a map of the district, which not only restores the external scene to the mind's eye, but casts a strong and fearful light —as we shall see presently—on the origin and course of the troubles of 1692. Mr. Upham and his sons have minutely examined the territory—tracing the old stone walls and the streams, fixing the gates, measuring distances, even verifying points of view, till the surrounding scenery has become as complete as could be desired. Between the church books and the parish and court records, the character, repute, ways, and manners of every conspicuous resident can be ascertained; and it may be said that nothing out of the common way happened to any man, woman, or child within the district which could remain unknown at this day, if any one wished to make it out. Mr. Upham has wished to make out the real story of the Witch Tragedy; and he has done it in such a way that his readers will doubtless agree that no more accurate piece of history has ever been written than the annals of this New England township.

For such a work, however, something more is required than the most minute delineation of the outward conditions of men and society; and in this higher department of his task Mr. Upham is above all anxious to obtain and dispense true light. The second part of his work treats of what may be called the spiritual scenery of the time. He exhibits the superstition of that age, when the belief in Satanic agency was the governing idea of religious life, and the most engrossing and pervading interest known to the Puritans of every country. Of the young and ignorant in the new settlement beyond the seas his researches have led him to write thus:

THE ACTORS IN THE TRAGEDY.

"However strange it seems, it is quite worthy of observation, that the actors in that tragedy, the 'afflicted children,' and other witnesses, in their various statements and operations, embraced about the whole circle of popular superstition. How those young country girls, some of them mere children, most of them wholly illiterate, could have become familiar with such fancies, to such an extent, is truly surprising. They acted out, and brought to bear with tremendous effect, almost all that can be found in the literature of that day, and the period preceding it, relating to such subjects. Images and visions which had been portrayed in tales of romance, and given interest to the pages of poetry, will be made by them, as we shall see, to throng the woods, flit through the air, and hover over the heads of a terrified court. The ghosts of murdered wives and children will play their parts with a vividness of representation and artistic skill of expression that have hardly been surpassed in scenic representations on the stage. In the Salem-witchcraft proceedings, the superstition of the middle ages was embodied in real action. All its extravagant absurdities and monstrosities appear in their application to human experience. We see what the effect has been, and must be, when the affairs of life, in courts of law and the relations of society, or the conduct or feelings of individuals, are suffered to be under the control of fanciful or mystical notions. When a whole people abandons the solid ground of common sense, overleaps the boundaries of human knowledge, gives itself up to wild reveries, and lets loose its passions without restraint, it presents a spectacle more terrific to behold, and becomes more destructive and disastrous, than any convulsion of mere material nature,—than tornado, conflagration, or earthquake." (Vol. i. p. 468.)

PHILOSOPHY OF THE DELUSION.

All this is no more than might have occurred to a thoughtful historian long years ago; but there is yet something else which it has been reserved for our generation to perceive, or at least to declare, without fear or hesitation. Mr. Upham may mean more than some people would in what he says of the new opening made by science into the dark depths of mystery covered by the term Witchcraft; for he is not only the brother-in-law but the intimate friend and associate of Dr.

Oliver Wendell Holmes, Professor of Anatomy and Physiology at Harvard University, and still better known to us, as he is at home, as the writer of the physiological tales, "Elsie Venner" and the "Guardian Angel," which have impressed the public as something new in the literature of fiction. It can not be supposed that Mr. Upham's view of the Salem Delusion would have been precisely what we find it here if he and Dr. Holmes had never met; and, but for the presence of the Professor's mind throughout the book, which is most fitly dedicated to him, its readers might have perceived less clearly the true direction in which to look for a solution of the mystery of the story, and its writer might have written something less significant in the place of the following paragraph:

"As showing how far the beliefs of the understanding, the perceptions of the senses, and the delusions of the imagination may be confounded, the subject belongs not only to theology and moral and political science, but to *physiology*, in its original and proper use, as embracing our whole nature; and the facts presented may help to conclusions relating to what is justly regarded as the great mystery of our being—the connection between the body and the mind." (Vol. i. p. viii.)

CHARACTER OF THE EARLY SETTLEMENT.

The settlement had its birth in 1620, the date of the charter granted by James I. to "the Governor and Company of Massachusetts Bay in New England." The first policy of the company was to attract families of good birth, position, education, and fortune, to take up considerable portions of land, introduce the best agriculture known, and facilitate the settling of the country. Hence the tone of manners, the social organization, and the prevalence of the military spirit, which the subsequent decline in the spirit of the community made it difficult for careless thinkers to understand. Not only did the wealth of this class of early settlers supply the district with roads and bridges, and clear the forest; it set up the pursuit of agriculture in the highest place, and encouraged intellectual pursuits, refined intercourse, and a loftier spirit of colonizing enterprise than can be looked for among immigrants whose energies are engrossed by the needs of the day. The mode of dress of the gentry of this class shows us something of their aspect in their new country, when prowling Indians were infesting the woods a stone's throw from their fences, and when the rulers of the community took it in turn with all their neighbors to act as scouts against the savages. George Corwin was thus dressed:

"A wrought flowing neckcloth, a sash covered with lace, a coat with short cuffs and reaching halfway between the wrist and elbow; the skirts in plaits below; an octagon ring and cane. The last two articles are still preserved. His inventory mentions 'a silver-laced cloth coat, a velvet ditto, a satin waistcoat embroidered with gold, a trooping scarf and silver hat-band, golden-topped and embroidered, and a silver-headed cane.'" (Vol. i. p. 98.)

This aristocratic element was in large proportion to the total number of settlers. It lifted up the next class to a position inferior only to its own by its connection with land. The farmers formed an order by themselves—not by having peculiar institutions, but through the dignity ascribed to agriculture. The yeomanry of Massachusetts hold their heads high to this day, and their fathers spoke proudly of themselves as "the farmers." They penetrated the forest in all directions, sat down beside the streams, and plowed up such level tracts as they found open to the sunshine; so that in a few years "the Salem Farms" constituted a well-defined territory, thinly peopled, but entirely appropriated. In due course parishes were formed round the outskirts of "Salem Farms," encroaching more or less in all directions, and reducing the area to that which was ultimately known as "Salem Village," in which some few of the original grants of five hundred acres or less remained complete, while others were divided among families or sold. Long before the date of the Salem Tragedy, the strifes which follow upon the acquisition of land had become common, and there was much ill-blood within the bounds of the City of Peace. The independence, the mode of life, and the pride of the yeomen made them excellent citizens, however, when war broke out with the Indians or with any other foe; and the military spirit of the aristocracy was well sustained by that of the farmers.

The dignity of the town had been early secured by the wisdom of the Company at home, which had committed to the people the government of the district in which they were placed; and every citizen felt himself, in his degree, concerned in the rule and good order of the society in which he lived; but the holders of land recognized no real equality between themselves and men of other callings, while the artisans and laborers were ambitious to obtain a place in the higher class

Artisans of every calling needed in a new society had been sent out from England by the Company; and when all the most energetic had acquired as much land as could be had in recompense for special services to the community—as so many acres for plowing up a meadow, so many for discovering minerals, so many for foiling an Indian raid,—and when the original grants had been broken up, and finally parceled out among sons and daughters, leaving no scope for new purchasers, the most ambitious of the adventurers applied for tracts in Maine, where they might play their part of First Families in a new settlement. The weaker, the more envious, the more ill-conditioned thus remained behind, to cavil at their prosperous neighbors, and spite them if they could. Here was an evident preparation for social disturbance, when opportunity for gratifying bad passions should arise.

FIRST CAUSES.

There had been a preparation for this stage in the temper with which the adventurers had arrived in the country, and the influences which at once operated upon them there. The politics and the religion in which they had grown up were gloomy and severe. Those who were not soured were sad; and, it should be remembered, they fully believed that Satan and his powers were abroad, and must be contended with daily and hourly, and in every transaction of life. In their new home they found little cheer from the sun and the common daylight; for the forest shrouded the entire land beyond the barren seashore. The special enemy, the Red Indian, always watching them and seeking his advantage of them, was not, in their view, a simple savage. Their clergy assured them that the Red Indians were worshipers and agents of Satan; and it is difficult to estimate the effect of this belief on the minds and tempers of those who were thinking of the Indians at every turn of daily life. The passion which is in the far West still spoken of as special, under the name of "Indian-hating," is a mingled ferocity and fanaticism quite inconceivable by quiet Christians, or perhaps by any but border adventurers; and this passion, kindled by the first demonstration of hostility on the part of the Massachusetts Red Man, grew and spread incessantly under the painful early experiences of colonial life. Every man had in turn to be scout, by day and night, in the swamp and in the forest; and every woman had to be on the watch in her husband's absence to save her babes from murderers and kidnappers. Whatever else they might want to be doing, even to supply their commonest needs, the citizens had first to station themselves within hail of each other all day, and at night to drive in their cattle among the dwellings, and keep watch by turns. Even on Sundays patrols were appointed to look to the public safety while the community were at church. The mothers carried their babes to the meeting-house, rather than venture to stay at home in the absence of husband and neighbors. One function of the Sabbath patrol indicates to us other sources of trouble. While looking for Indians, the patrol was to observe who was absent from worship, to mark what the absentees were doing, and to give information to the authorities. These patrols were chosen from the leading men of the community—the most active, vigilant, and sensible—and it is conceivable that much ill-will might have been accumulated in the hearts of not only the ne'er-do-weels, but timid and jealous and angry persons who were uneasy under this Sabbath inspection. Such ill-will had its day of triumph when the Salem Tragedy arrived at its catastrophe.

DEATH OF THE PATRIARCH.

The ordinary experience of life was singularly accelerated in that new state of society, though in the one particular of the age attained by the primitive adventurers, the community may be regarded as favored. Death made a great sweep of the patriarchs at last—shortly before the Tragedy—but an unusual proportion of elders presided over social affairs for seventy years after the date of the second charter. The chief seats in the meeting-house were filled by gray-haired men and women, rich or poor as might happen; and they were allowed to retain their places, whoever else might be shifted in the yearly "seating." The title "Landlord" distinguished the most dignified, and the eldest of each family of the "Old Planters;" a "Goodman" and "Goodwife" (abbreviated to "Goody") were titles of honor, as signifying heads of households. The old age of these venerable persons was carefully cherished; and when, as could not but happen, many of them departed near together, the mourning of the community was deep and bitter. Society seemed to be deprived of its parents, and in fear and grief it anticipated the impending calamity. Except in regard to these patriarchs, and their long old age, the pace of events was very rapid. Early marriages might be looked for in a society so youthful; but the rapid succession of second and subsequent marriages is a striking feature in the register. The most devoted affection seems to have had no effect in deferring a second marriage so long as a year. No time was lost in settling in life at first; families were large; and half-brothers and sisters abounded; and as they grew up they married on the portions which were given them, as a matter of course,—each having house, land, and plenishing, until at last the parents gave away all but a sufficiency for their own need or convenience, and went into the town or remained in the central mansion, turning over the land and its cares to the younger generation. When there was a failure of offspring, the practice of adoption seems to have been resorted to almost as a natural process, which, in such a state of society, it probably was.

GROWTH.

In the early days of the arts of life it is usual for the separate transactions of each day to be slow and cumbrous; but the experience of life may be rapid nevertheless. While traveling was a rough jog-trot, and forest-land took years to clear, and the harvest weeks to gather, property grew fast, marriages were precipitate and repeated, one generation trod on the heels of another, and the old folks complained that The Enemy made rapid conquest of the new territory which they had hoped he could not enter. When any work—of house-building, or harvesting, or nutting, or furnishing, or raising the wood-pile—had to be done, it was secured by assembling all the hands in the neighborhood, and turning the toil into a festive pleasure. We have all read of such "bees" in the rural districts of America down to the present day; and we can easily understand how the "goodmen" and "goodies" watched for the good and the evil which came out of such celebrations—the courtship and marriage, and the neighborly interest and good offices on the one hand, and the evil passions from disappointed hopes, envy, jealousy, tittle-tattle, rash judgment, and slander on the other. Much that was said, done, and inferred in such meetings as these found its way long afterward into the Tragedy at Salem. Mr. Upham depicts the inner side of the young social life of which the inquisitorial meeting-house and the courts were the black shadow:

"The people of the early colonial settlements had a private and interior life, as much as we have now, and the people of all ages and countries have had. It is common to regard them in no other light than as a severe, somber, and pleasure-abhorring generation. It was not so with them altogether. They had the same nature that we have. It was not all gloom and severity. They had their recreations, amusements, gayeties, and frolics. Youth was as buoyant with hope and gladness, love as warm and tender, mirth as natural to innocence, wit as sprightly, then as now. There was as much poetry and romance; the merry laugh enlivened the newly opened fields, and rang through the bordering woods as loud, jocund, and unrestrained as in these older and more crowded settlements. It is true that their theology was austere, and their policy, in Church and State, stern; but, in their modes of life, there were some features which gave peculiar opportunity to exercise and gratify a love of social excitement of a pleasurable kind." (Vol. i. p. 200.)

Except such conflicts as arose about the boundaries of estates when the General Court was remiss in making and enforcing its decisions, the first and greatest strifes related to Church matters and theological doctrines. The farmers had more lively minds, better informed as to law, and more exercised in reasoning and judging than their class are usually supposed to have; for there never was a time when lawsuits were not going forward about the area and the rights of some landed property or other; and intelligent men were called on to follow the course of litigation, if not to serve the community in office. Thus they were prepared for the strife when the operation of the two Churches pressed for settlement.

TROUBLE IN THE CHURCH.

The farmers in the rural district thenceforward to be called "Salem Village," desired to have a meeting-house and a minister of their own; but the town authorities insisted on taxing them for the religious establishment in Salem, from which they derived no benefit. In 1670, twenty of them petitioned to be set off as a parish, and allowed to provide a minister for themselves. In two years more the petition was granted, as a compromise for larger privileges; but there were restrictions which spoiled the grace of such concession as there was. One of these restrictions was that no minister was to be permanently settled without the permission of the old Church to proceed to his ordination. Endless trouble arose out of this provision. The men who had contributed the land, labor, and material for the meeting-house, and the maintenance for the pastor, naturally desired to be free in their choice of their minister, while the Church authorities in Salem considered themselves responsible for the maintenance of true doctrine, and for leaving no opening for Satan to enter the fold in the form of heresy, or any kind or degree of dissent. Their fathers, the first settlers, had made the colony too hot for one of their most virtuous and distinguished citizens, because he had views of his own on Infant Baptism; they had brought him to judgment, magistrate and church member as he was, for not having presented his infant child at the font; he had sold his estates and gone away. If such a citizen as Townsend Bishop was thus lost to their society, how could the guardians of religion surrender their control over any church or pastor within their reach? They had spiritual charge of a community which had made its abode on the American shore for the single purpose of living its own religious life in its own way; and no dissent or modification from within could be permitted, any more than intrusion or molestation from without. Between the ecclesiastical view on the one hand, and the civil view on the other, there was small chance of harmony between town and village, or between pastor, flock, and the overseers of both. The great point on which they were all agreed was that they were all in special danger from the extreme malice of Satan, who, foiled in Puritan England, was bent on revenge in America, and was visibly and audibly present in the settlement, seeking whom he might devour.

Quarreling began with the appearance of the first minister, a young Mr. Bayley, who was appointed from year to year, but never ordained the pastor till 1679, when the authorities of Salem tried to force him upon the people of Salem Village in the face of strong opposition. The farmers disregarded the orders issued from the town, and managed their religious affairs by general meetings of their own congregation; and at length Mr. Bayley retired, leaving the society in a much worse temper than he had found on his arrival. A handsome gift of land was settled upon him, in acknowledgment of his services; he quitted the ministry, and practiced medicine in Roxbury till his death, nearly thirty years afterward.

REV. MR. BURROUGHS.

His partisans were enemies of his successor, of course, Mr. Burroughs was a man of even distinguished excellence in the pastoral relation, in days when risks from Indians made that duty as perilous as the career of the soldier in war time; but his flock were divided, church business was neglected, he was allowed to fall into want. He withdrew, was recalled to settle accounts, was arrested for debt in full meeting—the debt being for the funeral expenses of his wife—was absolved from all blame under the cruel neglect he had experienced—and left the Village. Before he could hear in his remote home in Maine what was doing at Salem in the first days of the Witch Tragedy, he was summoned to his old neighborhood, was charged with sorcery on the most childish and absurd testimony conceivable, and executed in August, 1692. One of the witnesses—a young girl morbid in body and mind—poured out her remorse to him the day before his death. He, believing her a victim of Satan, forgave her, prayed with her, and died honored and beloved by all who were not under the curse of the bigotry of the time.

DEODAT LAWSON.

The third minister was one Deodat Lawson, who is notable—besides his learning—for his Sermon on the Devil, and for some mournful mystery about his end. Of his last days there is nothing known but that there was something woeful in them; but his sermon, preached at the commencement of the outbreak in Salem, remains to us. It was published in America, and then widely circulated in England. It met the popular craving for light about Satan and his doings; and thus, between its appropriateness to the time and occasion, and the learning and ability which it manifested, it produced an extraordinary effect in its day. In ours it is an instructive evidence of the extent to which "knowledge falsely so called" may operate on the mind of society, in the absence of science, and before the time has arrived for a clear understanding of the nature of knowledge and the conditions of its attainment. Mr. Lawson bore a part in the Salem Tragedy, and then went to England, where we hear of him from Calamy as "the unhappy Mr. Deodat Lawson," and he disappears.

PARRIS—A MALIGNANT.

The fourth and last of the ministers of Salem Village, before the Tragedy, was the Mr. Parris who played the most conspicuous part in it. He must have been a man of singular shamelessness, as well as remarkable selfishness, craft, ruthlessness, and withal imprudence. He **began his operations with sharp bargaining about his stipend, and** sharp practice in appropriating the house and land assigned for the use of successive pastors. He wrought diligently under the stimulus of his ambition till he got his meeting-house sanctioned as a true church, and himself ordained as the first pastor of Salem Village. This was in 1689. He immediately launched out into such an exercise of priestly power as could hardly be exceeded under any form of church government; he set his people by the ears on every possible occasion and on every possible pretense; he made his church a scandal in the land for its brawls and controversies; and on him rests the responsibility of the disease and madness which presently turned his parish into a hell, and made it famous for the murder of the wisest, gentlest, and purest Christians it contained. [This man Parris must have had an inferior intellect, small Conscientiousness, Benevolence, and Veneration; large Firmness, Self-Esteem, Combativeness, Destructiveness, and Acquisitiveness.]

A PROTEAN DEVIL.

Before we look at his next proceeding, however, we must bring into view one or two facts essential to the understanding of the case. We have already observed on the universality of the belief in the ever-present agency of Satan in that region and that special season. In the woods the Red Men were his agents—living in and for his service and his worship. In the open country, Satan himself was seen, as a black horse, a black dog, as a tall, dark stranger, as a raven, a wolf, a cat, etc. Strange incidents happened there as everywhere—odd bodily affections and mental movements; and when devilish influences are watched for, they are sure to be seen. Everybody was prepared for manifestations of witchcraft from the first landing in the Bay; and there had been more and more cases, not only rumored, but brought under investigation, for some years before the final outbreak.

This suggests the next consideration: that the generation concerned had no "alternative" explanation within their reach, when perplexed by unusual appearances or actions of body or mind. They believed themselves perfectly certain about the Devil and his doings; and his agency was the only solution of their difficulties, while it was a very complete one. They thought they knew that his method of working was by human agents, whom he had won over and bound to his service. They had all been brought up to believe this; and they never thought of doubting it.

STATE OF PHYSIOLOGY.

The very conception of science had then scarcely begun to be formed in the minds of the wisest men of the time; and if it had been, who was there to suggest that the handful of pulp contained in the human skull, and the soft string of marrow in the spine, and cobweb lines of nerves, apparently of no more account than the hairs of the head, could transmit thoughts, emotions, passions—all the scenery of the spiritual world! For two hundred years more there was no effectual recognition of anything of the sort. At the end of those two centuries anatomists themselves were slicing the brain like a turnip, to see what was inside it,—not dreaming of the leading facts of its structure, nor of the inconceivable delicacy of its organization. After half a century of knowledge of the main truth in regard to the brain, and nearly that period of study of its organization, by every established medical authority in the civilized world, we are still perplexed and baffled at every turn of the inquiry into the relations of body and mind. How, then, can we make sufficient allowance for the effects of ignorance in a community where theology was the main interest in life, where science was yet unborn, and where all the influences of the period concurred to produce and aggravate superstitions and bigotries which now seem scarcely credible?

[The reviewer appears to be a half believer in Phrenology, and yet unwilling to acknowledge his indebtedness to its teachers for the light he has received in the organization and phenomena of the brain.]

WILLIAM PENN AS A PRECEDENT.

There had been misery enough caused by persecutions for witchcraft within living memory to have warned Mr. Parris, one would think, how he carried down his people into those troubled waters again; but at that time such trials were regarded by society as trials for murder are by us, and not as anything surprising except from the degree of wickedness. William Penn presided at the trial of two Swedish women in Philadelphia for this gravest of crimes; and it was only by the accident of a legal informality that they escaped, the case being regarded with about the same feeling as we experienced a year or two ago when the murderess of infants, Charlotte Winsor, was saved from hanging by a doubt of the law. If the crime spread—as it usually did —the municipal governments issued an order for a day of fasting and humiliation, "in consideration of the extent to which Satan prevails amongst us in respect of witchcraft." Among the prosecutions which followed on such observances there was one here and there which turned out, too late, to have been a mistake. This kind of discovery might be made an occasion for more fasting and humiliation; but it seems to have had no effect in inducing caution or suggesting self-distrust. Mr. Parris and his partisans must have been aware that on occasion of the last great spread of witchcraft, the magistrates and the General Court had set aside the verdict of the jury in one case of wrongful accusation, and that there were other instances in which the general heart and conscience were cruelly wounded and oppressed, under the conviction that the wisest and saintliest woman in the community had been made away with by malice, at least as much as mistaken zeal.

The wife of one of the most honored and prominent citizens of Boston, and the sister of the Deputy Governor of Massachusetts, Mrs. Hibbins, might have been supposed safe from the gallows, while she walked in uprightness, and all holiness and gentleness of living. But her husband died; and the pack of fanatics sprang upon her, and tore her to pieces—name and fame, fortune, life, and everything. She was hanged in 1656, and the farmers of Salem Village and their pastor were old enough to know, in Mr. Parris' time, how the "famous Mr. Norton," an eminent pastor, "once said at his own table",—before clergymen and elders—"that one of their magistrates' wives was hanged for a witch, only for having more wit than her neighbors;" and to be aware that in Boston "a deep feeling of resentment" against her persecutors rankled in the minds of some of her citizens; and that they afterward "observed solemn marks of Providence set upon those who were very forward to condemn her." The story of Mrs. Hibbins, as told in the book before us, with the brief and simple comment of her own pleading in court, and the codicil to her will, is so piteous and so fearful, that it is difficult to imagine how any clergyman could countenance a similar procedure before the memory of the execution had died out, and could be supported in his course by officers of his church, and at length by the leading clergy of the district, the magistrates, the physicians, "and devout women not a few."

[Here are evidences of large Cautiousness, fear, and timidity, with the vivid imagination of untrained childhood.]

PHENOMENA OF WITCHERY.

In the interval between the execution of Mrs. Hibbins and the outbreak at Salem an occasional breeze arose against some unpopular member of society. If a man's ox was ill, if the beer ran out of the cask, if the butter would not come in the churn, if a horse shied or was restless when this or that man or woman was in sight; and if a woman knew when her neighbors were talking about her (which was Mrs. Hibbins' most indisputable proof of connection with the devil), rumors got about of Satanic intercourse; men and women made deposition that six or seven years before, they had seen the suspected person yawn in church, and had observed a "devil's teat" distinctly visible under his tongue; and children told of bears coming to them in the night, and of a buzzing devil in the humble-bee, and of a cat on the bed thrice as big as an ordinary cat. But the authorities, on occasion, exercised some caution. They fined one accused person for telling a lie, instead of treating his bragging as inspiration of the devil. They induced timely confession, or discovered flaws in the evidence, as often as they could; so that there was less disturbance in the immediate neighborhood than in some other parts of the province. Where the Rev. Mr. Parris went, however, there was no more peace and quiet, no more privacy in the home, no more harmony in the church, no more good-will or good manners in society.

As soon as he was ordained he put perplexing questions about baptism before the farmers, who rather looked to him for guidance in such matters than expected to be exercised in theological mysteries which they had never studied. He exposed to the congregation the spiritual conflicts of individual members who were too humble for their own comfort. He preached and prayed incessantly about his own wrongs and the slights he suffered, in regard to his salary and supplies; and entered satirical notes in the margin of the church records; so that he was as abundantly discussed from house to house, and from end to end of his parish, as he himself could have desired. In the very crisis of the discontent, and when his little world was expecting to see him dismissed, he saved himself, as we ourselves have of late seen other persons relieve themselves under stress of mind and circumstances, by a rush into the world of spirits.

Four years previously, a poor immigrant, a Catholic Irishwoman, had been hanged in Boston for bewitching four children, named Goodwin—one of whom, a girl of thirteen, had sorely tried a reverend man, less irascible than Mr. Parris, but nearly as excitable. The tricks that the little girl played the Reverend Cotton Mather, when he endeavored to exorcise the evil spirits, are precisely such as are familiar to us, in cases which are common in the practice of every physician. If we can not pretend to explain them—in the true sense of explaining—that is, referring them to an ascertained law of nature, we know what to look for under certain conditions, and are aware that it is the brain and nervous system that is implicated in these phenomena, and not the Prince of Darkness and his train. Cotton Mather had no alternative at his disposal. Satan or nothing was his only choice. He published the story, with all its absurd details; and it was read in almost every house in the Province. At Salem it wrought with fatal effect, because there was a pastor close by well qualified to make the utmost mischief out of it.

[In cases of *hysteria*, the phenomena are sometimes so remarkable, that one is disposed to attribute their cause to influences beyond nature.]

PARRIS AND HIS "CIRCLE."

Mr. Parris had lived in the West Indies for some years, and had brought several slaves with him to Salem. One of these, an Indian named John, and Tituba his wife, seem to have been full of the gross superstitions of their people, and of the frame and temperament best adapted for the practices of demonology. In such a state of affairs the pastor actually formed, or allowed to be formed, a society of young girls between the ages of eight and eighteen to meet in his parsonage, strongly resembling those " circles " in the America of our time which have filled the lunatic asylums with thousands of victims of " spiritualist " visitations. It seems that these young persons were laboring under strong nervous excitement, which was encouraged rather than repressed by the means employed by their spiritual director. Instead of treating them as the subjects of morbid delusion, Mr. Parris regarded them as the victims of external diabolical influence; and this influence was, strangely enough, supposed to be exercised, on the evidence of the children themselves, by some of the most pious and respectable members of the community.

We need not describe the course of events. In the dull life of the country, the excitement of the proceedings in the "circle" was welcome, no doubt; and it was always on the increase. Whatever trickery there might be—and no doubt there was plenty; whatever excitement to hysteria, whatever actual sharpening of common faculties, it is clear that there was more; and those who have given due and dispassionate attention to the processes of mesmerism and their effects can have no difficulty in understanding the reports handed down of what these young creatures did, and said, and saw, under peculiar conditions of the nervous system. When the physicians of the district could see no explanation of the ailments of " the afflicted children " but " the evil hand," no doubt could remain to those who consulted them of these agonies being the work of Satan. The matter was settled at once. But Satan can work only through human agents; and who were his instruments for the affliction of these children? Here was the opening through which calamity rushed in; and for half a year this favored corner of the godly land of New England was turned into a hell. The more the children were stared at and pitied, the bolder they grew in their vagaries, till at last they broke through the restraints of public worship, and talked nonsense to the minister in the pulpit, and profaned the prayers. Mr. Parris assembled all the divines he could collect at his parsonage, and made his troop go through their performances—the result of which was a general groan over the manifest presence of the Evil One, and a passionate intercession for "the afflicted children."

[These afflicted children of Salem, in 1690, were kindred to the numerous "mediums" of 1869. In the former, ignorance ascribed their actions and revelations to the devil, who bewitched certain persons. Now, we simply have the more innocent "communications" from where and from whom you like.]

THE INQUISITIONS.—SARAH GOOD.

The first step toward relief was to learn who it was that had stricken them; and the readiest means that occurred was to ask this question of the children themselves. At first, they named no names, or what they said was not disclosed; but there was soon an end of all such delicacy. The first symptoms had occurred in November, 1691; and the first public examination of witches took place on the 1st of March following. We shall cite as few of the cases as will suffice for our purpose; for they are exceedingly painful; and there is something more instructive for us in the spectacle of the consequences, and in the suggestions of the story, than in the scenery of persecution and murder.

In the first group of accused persons was one Sarah Good, a weak, ignorant, poor, despised woman, whose equally weak and ignorant husband had forsaken her, and left her to the mercy of evil tongues. He had called her an enemy to all good, and had said that if she was not a witch, he feared she would be one shortly. Her assertions under examination were that she knew nothing about the matter; that she had hurt nobody, nor employed anybody to hurt another; that she served God; and that the God she served was He who made heaven and earth. It appears, however, that she believed in the reality of the "affliction;" for she ended by accusing a fellow-prisoner of having hurt the children. The report of the examination, noted at the time by two of the heads of the congregation, is inane and silly beyond belief; yet the celebration was unutterably solemn to the assembled crowd of fellow-worshipers; and it sealed the doom of the community, in regard to peace and good repute.

A CHILD WITCH.

Mrs. Good was carried to jail. Not long after her little daughter Dorcas, aged four years, was apprehended at the suit of the brothers Putnam, chief citizens of Salem. There was plenty of testimony produced of bitings and chokings and pinchings inflicted by this infant; and she was committed to prison, and probably, as Mr. Upham says, fettered with the same chains which bound her mother. Nothing short of chains could keep witches from flying away; and they were chained at the cost of the state, when they could not pay for their own irons. As these poor creatures were friendless and poverty-stricken, it is some comfort to find the jailer charging for "two blankets for Sarah Good's child," costing ten shillings.

What became of little Dorcas, with her healthy looks and natural childlike spirits, noticed by her accusers, we do not learn. Her mother lay in chains till the 29th of June, when she was brought out to receive sentence. She was hanged on the 19th of July, after having relieved her heart by vehement speech of some of the passion which weighed upon it. She does not seem to have been capable of much thought

One of the accusers was convicted of a flagrant lie, in the act of giving testimony: but the narrator, Hutchinson, while giving the fact, treats it as of no consequence, because Sir Matthew Hale and the jury of his court were satisfied with the condemnation of a witch under precisely the same circumstances. The parting glimpse we have of this first victim is dismally true on the face of it. It is most characteristic.

"Sarah Good appears to have been an unfortunate woman, having been subject to poverty, and consequent sadness and melancholy. But she was not wholly broken in spirit. Mr. Noyes, at the time of her execution, urged her very strenuously to confess. Among other things, he told her 'she was a witch, and that she knew she was a witch.' She was conscious of her innocence, and felt that she was oppressed, outraged, trampled upon, and about to be murdered, under the forms of law; and her indignation was roused against her persecutors. She could not bear in silence the cruel aspersion; and although she was about to be launched into eternity, the torrent of her feelings could not be restrained, but burst upon the head of him who uttered the false accusation. 'You are a liar,' said she. 'I am no more a witch than you are a wizard; and if you take away my life, God will give you blood to drink.' Hutchinson says that, in his day, there was a tradition among the people of Salem, and it has descended to the present time, that the manner of Mr. Noyes' death strangely verified the prediction thus wrung from the incensed spirit of the dying woman. He was exceedingly corpulent, of a plethoric habit, and died of an internal hemorrhage, bleeding profusely at the mouth." (Vol. ii. p. 269.)

When she had been in her grave nearly twenty years, her representatives—little Dorcas perhaps for one—were presented with thirty pounds sterling, as a grant from the Crown, as compensation for the mistake of hanging her without reason and against evidence.

THE TOWNE SISTERS.

In the early part of the century, a devout family named Towne were living at Great Yarmouth, in the English county of Norfolk. About the time of the King's execution they emigrated to Massachusetts. William Towne and his wife carried with them two daughters; and another daughter and a son were born to them afterward in Salem. The three daughters were baptized at long intervals, and the eldest, Rebecca, must have been at least twenty years older than Sarah, and a dozen or more years older than Mary. A sketch of the fate of these three sisters contains within it the history of a century.

On the map which Mr. Upham presents us with, one of the most conspicuous estates is an inclosure of 300 acres, which had a significant story of its own—too long for us to enter upon. We need only say that there had been many strifes about this property—fights about boundaries, and stripping of timber, and a series of lawsuits. Yet, from 1678 onward, the actual residents in the mansion had lived in peace, taking no notice of wrangles which did not, under the conditions of purchase, affect them, but only the former proprietor. The frontispiece of Mr. Upham's book shows us what the mansion of an opulent landowner was like in the early days of the colony. It is the portrait of the house in which the eldest daughter of William Towne was living at the date of the Salem Tragedy.

Rebecca, then the aged wife of Francis Nurse, was a great-grandmother, and between seventy and eighty years of age. No old age could have had a more lovely aspect than hers. Her husband was, as he had always been, devoted to her, and the estate was a colony of sons and daughters, and their wives and husbands; for 'Landlord Nurse' had divided his land between his four sons and three sons-in-law, and had built homesteads for them all as they married and settled. Mrs. Nurse was in full activity of faculty, except being somewhat deaf from age; and her health was good, except for certain infirmities of long standing, which it required the zeal and the malice of such a divine as Mr. Parris to convert into "devil's marks." As for her repute in the society of which she was the honored head, we learn what it was by the testimony supplied by forty persons—neighbors and householders—who were inquired of in regard to their opinion of her in the day of her sore trial. Some of them had known her above forty years; they had seen her bring up a large family in uprightness; they had remarked the beauty of her Christian profession and conduct; and had never heard or observed any evil of her. This was Rebecca, the eldest.

The next, Mary, was now fifty-eight years old, the wife of "Goodman Easty," the owner of a large farm. She had seven children, and was living in ease and welfare of every sort when overtaken by the same calamity as her sister Nurse. Sarah, the youngest, had married twice. Her present husband was Peter Cloyse, whose name occurs in the parish records, and in various depositions which show that he was a prominent citizen. When Mr. Parris was publicly complaining of neglect in respect of firewood for the parsonage, and of lukewarmness on the part of the hearers of his services, "Landlord Nurse" was a member of the committee who had to deal with him; and his relatives were probably among the majority who were longing for Mr. Parris' apparently inevitable departure. In these circumstances, it was not altogether surprising that "the afflicted children" trained in the parsonage parlor, ventured, after their first successes, to name the honored "Goody Nurse" as one of the allies lately acquired by Satan. They saw her here, there, everywhere, when she was sitting quietly at home; they saw her biting the black servants, choking, pinching, pricking women and children; and if she was examined, devil's marks would doubtless be found upon her. She *was* examined by a jury of her own sex. Neither the testimony of her sisters and daughters as to her infirmities, nor the disgust of decent neighbors, nor the commonest suggestions of reason and feeling, availed to save her from the injury of being reported to have what the witnesses were looking for.

We have a glimpse of her in her home when the first conception of her impending fate opened upon her. Four esteemed persons, one of whom was her brother-in-law, Mr. Cloyse, made the following deposition, in the prospect of the victim being dragged before the public:

"We whose names are underwritten being desired to go to Goodman Nurse, his house, to speak with his wife, and to tell her that several of the afflicted persons mentioned her; and accordingly we went, and we found her in a weak and low condition in body as she told us, and had been sick almost a week. And we asked how it was otherwise with her; and she said she blessed God for it, she had more of his presence in this sickness than sometimes she have had, but not so much as she desired; but she would, with the Apostle, press forward to the mark; and many other places of Scripture to the like purpose. And then of her own accord she began to speak of the affliction that was among them, and in particular of Mr. Parris his family, and how she was grieved for them, though she had not been to see them, by reason of fits that she formerly used to have; for people said it was awful to behold: but she pitied them with all her heart, and went to God for them. But she said she heard that there was persons spoke of that were as innocent as she was, she believed; and after much to this purpose, we told her we heard that she was spoken of also. 'Well, she said, 'if it be so, the will of the Lord be done:' she sat still awhile being as it were amazed; and then she said, 'Well, as to this thing I am as innocent as the child unborn; but surely,' she said, 'what sin hath God found out in me unrepented of, that he should lay such an affliction upon me in my old age?' and, according to our best observation, we could not discern that she knew what we came for before we told her. ISRAEL PORTER, DANIEL ANDREW, ELIZABETH PORTER, PETER CLOYSE."

On the 22d of March she was brought into the thronged meeting-house to be accused before the magistrates, and to answer as she best could. We must pass over those painful pages, where nonsense, spasms of hysteria, new and strange to their worships, cunning, cruelty, blasphemy, indecency, turned the house of prayer into a hell for the time. The aged woman could explain nothing. She simply asserted her innocence, and supposed that some evil spirit was at work. One thing more she could do—she could endure with calmness malice and injustice which are too much for our composure at a distance of nearly two centuries. She felt the *animus* of her enemies, and she pointed out how they perverted whatever she said; but no impatient word escaped her. She was evidently as perplexed as anybody present. When weary and disheartened, and worn out with the noise and the numbers and the hysterics of the "afflicted," her head drooped on one shoulder. Immediately all the "afflicted" had twisted necks, and rude hands seized her head to set it upright, "lest other necks should be broken by her ill offices." Everything went against her, and the result was what had been hoped by the agitators. The venerable matron was carried to jail and put in irons.

DEPOSITIONS OF PARRIS AND HIS TOOLS.

Now Mr. Parris' time had arrived, and he broadly accused her of murder, employing for the purpose a fitting instrument—Mrs. Ann Putnam, the mother of one of the afflicted children, and herself of highly nervous temperament, undisciplined mind, and absolute devotedness to her pastor. Her deposition, preceded by a short one of Mr. Parris, will show the quality of the evidence on which judicial murder was inflicted:

"Mr. Parris gave in a deposition against her; from which it appears, that, a certain person being sick, Mercy Lewis was sent for. She was struck dumb on entering the chamber. She was asked to hold up her hand if she saw any of the witches afflicting the patient. Presently she held up her hand, then fell into a trance; and after a while, coming to herself, said that she saw the spectre of Goody Nurse and Goody Carrier having hold of the head of the sick man. Mr. Parris swore to this statement with the utmost confidence in Mercy's declarations." (Vol. ii. p. 275.)

"The deposition of Ann Putnam, the wife of Thomas Putnam, aged about thirty years, who testifieth and saith, that on March 18, 1692, I being wearied out in helping to tend my poor afflicted child and maid, about the middle of the afternoon I lay me down on the bed to take a little rest; and immediately I was almost pressed and choked to death, that had it not been for the mercy of a gracious God and the help of those that were with me, I could not have lived many moments; and presently I saw the apparition of Martha Corey, who did torture me so as I can not express, ready to tear me all to pieces, and then departed from me a little while; but, before I could recover strength or well take breath, the apparition of Martha Corey fell upon me again with dreadful tortures, and hellish temptation to go along with her. And she also brought to me a little red book in her hand, and a black pen, urging me vehemently to write in her book; and several times that day she did most grievously torture me, almost ready to kill me. And on the 19th of March, Martha Corey again appeared to me; and also Rebecca Nurse, the wife of Francis Nurse, Sr.; and they both did torture me a great many times this day, with such tortures as no tongue can express, because I would not yield to their hellish temptations, that, had I not been upheld by an Almighty arm, I could not have lived while night. The 20th of March, being Sabbath-day, I had a great deal of respite between my fits. 21st of March being the day of the examination of Martha Corey, I had not many fits, though I was very weak; my strength being, as I thought, almost gone; but, on 22d of March, 1692, the apparition of Rebecca Nurse did again set upon me in a most dreadful manner, very early in the morning, as soon as it was well light. And now she appeared to me only in her shift, and brought a little red book in her hand, urging me vehemently to write in her book; and, because I would not yield to her hellish temptations, she threatened to tear my soul out of my body, blasphemously denying the blessed God, and the power of the Lord Jesus Christ to save my soul; and denying several places of Scripture, which I told her of, to repel her hellish temptations. And for near two hours together, at this time, the apparition of Rebecca Nurse did tempt and torture me, and also the greater part of this day, with but very little respite. 23d of March, am again afflicted by the apparitions of Rebecca Nurse and Martha Corey, but chiefly by Rebecca Nurse. 24th of March, being the day of the examination of Rebecca Nurse, I was several times afflicted in the morning by the apparition of Rebecca Nurse, but most dreadfully tortured by her in the time of her examination, insomuch that the honored magistrates gave my husband leave to carry me out of the meeting-house; and, as soon as I was carried out of the meeting-house doors, it pleased Almighty God, for his free grace and mercy's sake, to deliver me out of the paws of those roaring lions, and jaws of those tearing bears, that, ever since that time, they have not had power so to afflict me until this May 31, 1692. At the same moment that I was hearing my evidence read by the honored magistrates, to take my oath, I was again re-assaulted and tortured by my before-mentioned tormentor, Rebecca Nurse." "The testimony of Ann Putnam, Jr., witnesseth and saith, that, being in the room where her mother was afflicted, she saw Martha Corey, Sarah Cloyse, and Rebecca Nurse, or their apparitions, upon her mother."

"Mrs. Ann Putnam made another deposition under oath at the same trial, which shows that she was determined to overwhelm the prisoner by the multitude of her charges. She says that Rebecca Nurse's apparition declared to her that 'she had killed Benjamin Houlton, John Fuller, and Rebecca Shepherd;' and that she and her sister Cloyse, and Edward Bishop's wife, had killed young John Putnam's child; and she further deposed as followeth: 'Immediately there did appear to me six children in winding-sheets, which called me aunt, which did most grievously affright me; and they told me that they were my sister Baker's children of Boston; and that Goody Nurse, and Mistress Corey of Charlestown, and an old deaf woman at Boston, had murdered them, and charged me to go and tell these things to the magistrates, or else they would tear me to pieces, for their blood did cry for vengeance. Also there appeared to me my own sister Bayley and three of her children in winding-sheets, and told me that Goody Nurse had murdered them.'" (Vol. ii. p. 278.)

All the efforts made to procure testimony against the venerable gentlewoman's character issued in a charge that she had so "railed at" a neighbor for allowing his pigs to get into her field that, some short time after, early in the morning, he had a sort of fit in his own entry, and languished in health from that day, and died in a fit at the end of the summer. "He departed this life by a cruel death," murdered by Goody Nurse. The jury did not consider this ground enough for hanging the old lady, who had been the ornament of their church and the glory of their village and its society. Their verdict was "Not Guilty." Not for a moment, however, could the prisoner and her family hope that their trial was over. The outside crowd clamored; the "afflicted" howled and struggled; one judge declared himself dissatisfied; another promised to have her indicted anew; and the Chief Justice pointed out a phrase of the prisoner's which might be made to signify that she was one of the accused gang in guilt, as well as in jeopardy. It might really seem as if the authorities were all driveling together, when we see the ingenuity and persistence with which they discussed those three words, "of our company." Her remonstrance ought to have moved them:

"I intended no otherwise than as they were prisoners with us, and therefore did then, and yet do, judge them not legal evidence against their fellow-prisoners. And I being something hard of hearing and full of grief, none informing me how the Court took up my words, therefore had no opportunity to declare what I intended when I said they were of our company." (Vol. ii. p. 285.)

The foreman of the jury would have taken the favorable view of this matter, and have allowed full consideration, while other jurymen were eager to recall the mistake of their verdict; but the prisoner's silence, from failing to hear when she was expected to explain, turned the foreman against her, and caused him to declare, "whereupon these words were to me a principal evidence against her." Still, it seemed too monstrous to hang her. After her condemnation, the Governor reprieved her; probably on the ground of the illegality of setting aside the first verdict of the jury, in the absence of any new evidence. But the outcry against mercy was so fierce that the Governor withdrew his reprieve.

GOODY NURSE'S EXCOMMUNICATION.

On the next Sunday there was a scene in the church, the record of which was afterward annotated by the church members in a spirit of grief and humiliation. After sacrament the elders propounded to the church, and the congregation unanimously agreed, that Sister Nurse, being convicted as a witch by the court, should be excommunicated in the afternoon of the same day. The place was thronged; the reverend elders were in the pulpit; the deacons presided below; the sheriff and his officers brought in the witch, and led her up the broad aisle, her chains clanking as she moved. As she stood in the middle of the aisle, the Reverend Mr. Noyes pronounced her sentence of expulsion from the Church on earth, and from all hope of salvation hereafter. As she had given her soul to Satan, she was delivered over to him for ever. She was aware that every eye regarded her with horror and hate, unapproached under any other circumstances; but it appears that she was able to sustain it. She was still calm and at peace on that day, and during the fortnight of final waiting. When the time came, she traversed the streets of Salem between houses in which she had been an honored guest, and surrounded by well-known faces; and then there was the hard task, for her aged limbs, of climbing the rocky and steep path on Witches' Hill to the place where the gibbets stood in a row, and the hangman was waiting for her, and for Sarah Good, and several more of whom Salem chose to be rid that day. It was the 19th of July, 1692. The bodies were put out of the way on the hill, like so many dead dogs; but this one did not remain there long. By pious hands it was—nobody knew when—brought home to the domestic cemetery, where the next generation pointed out the grave, next to her husband's, and surrounded by those of her children. As for her repute, Hutchinson, the historian, tells us that even excommunication could not permanently disgrace her. "Her life and conversation had been such, that the remembrance thereof, in a short time after, wiped off all the reproach occasioned by the civil or ecclesiastical sentence against her." (Vol. ii. p. 292.)

[Great God! and is this the road our ancestors had to travel in their pilgrimage in quest of freedom and Christianity? Are these the fruits of the misunderstood doctrine of total depravity?]

Thus much comfort her husband had till he died in 1695. In a little while none of his eight children remained unmarried, and he wound up his affairs. He gave over the homestead to his son Samuel, and divided all he had among the others, reserving only a mare and her saddle, some favorite articles of furniture, and £14 a year, with a right to call on his children for any further amount that might be needful. He made no will, and his children made no difficulties, but tended his latter days, and laid him in his own ground, when at seventy-seven years old he died.

In 1711, the authorities of the Province, sanctioned by the Council of Queen Anne, proposed such reparation as their heart and conscience suggested. They made a grant to the representatives of Rebecca Nurse of £25! In the following year something better was done, on the petition of the son Samuel who inhabited the homestead. A church meeting was called; the facts of the excommunication of twenty years before were recited, and a reversal was proposed, "the General Court having taken off the attainder, and the testimony on which she was convicted being not now so satisfactory to ourselves and others as it was generally in that hour of darkness and temptation." The remorseful congregation blotted out the record in the church book, "humbly requesting that the merciful God would pardon whatsoever sin, error, or mistake was in the application of that censure, and of the whole affair, through our merciful High Priest, who knoweth how to have compassion on the ignorant, and those that are out of the way." (Vol. ii. p. 483.)

MARY EASTY.

Such was the fate of Rebecca, the eldest of the three sisters. Mary, the next—once her playmate on the sands of Yarmouth, in the old country—was her companion to the last, in love and destiny. Mrs. Easty was arrested, with many other accused persons, on the 21st of April, while her sister was in jail in irons. The testimony against her was a mere repetition of the charges of torturing, strangling, pricking, and pinching Mr. Parris' young friends, and rendering them dumb, or blind, or amazed. Mrs. Easty was evidently so astonished and perplexed by the assertions of the children, that the magistrates inquired of the voluble witnesses whether they might not be mistaken. As they were positive, and Mrs. Easty could say only that she supposed it was "a bad spirit," but did not know "whether it was witchcraft or not," there was nothing to be done but to send her to prison and put her in irons. The next we hear of her is, that on the 18th of May she was free. The authorities, it seems, would not detain her on such evidence as was offered. She was at large for two days, and no more. The convulsions and tortures of the children returned instantly, on the news being told of Goody Easty being abroad again; and the ministers, and elders, and deacons, and all the zealous antagonists of Satan went to work so vigorously to get up a fresh case, that they bore down all before them. Mercy Lewis was so near death under the hands of Mrs. Easty's apparition that she was crying out "Dear Lord! receive my soul!" and thus there was clearly no time to be lost; and this choking and convulsion, says an eminent citizen, acting as a witness, "occurred very often until such time as we understood Mary Easty was laid in irons."

There she was lying when her sister Nurse was tried, excommunicated, and executed; and to the agony of all this was added the arrest of her sister Sarah, Mrs. Cloyse. But she had such strength as kept her serene up to the moment of her death on the gibbet on the 22d of September following. We would fain give, if we had room, the petition of the two sisters, Mrs. Easty and Mrs. Cloyse, to the court, when their trial was pending; but we can make room only for the last clause of its reasoning and remonstrance.

"Thirdly, that the testimony of witches, or such as are afflicted as is supposed by witches, may not be improved to condemn us without other legal evidence concurring. We hope the honored Court and jury will be so tender of the lives of such as we are, who have for many years lived under the unblemished reputation of Christianity, as not to condemn them without a fair and equal hearing of what may be said for us as well as against us. And your poor suppliants shall be bound always to pray, etc." (Vol. ii. p. 326.)

Still more affecting is the Memorial of Mrs. Easty when under sentence of death and fully aware of the hopelessness of her case. She addresses the judges, the magistrates, and the reverend ministers, imploring them to consider what they are doing, and how far their course in regard to accused persons is consistent with the principles and rules of justice. She asks nothing for herself; she is satisfied with her own innocency, and certain of her doom on earth and her hope in heaven. What she desires is to induce the authorities to take time, to use caution in receiving and strictness in sifting testimony; and so shall they ascertain the truth, and absolve the innocent, the blessing of God being upon their conscientious endeavors. We do not know of any effect produced by her warning and remonstrance; but we find her case estimated, twenty years afterward, as meriting a compensation of £20! [About one hundred dollars.] Before setting forth from the jail to the Witches' Hill, on the day of her death, she serenely bade farewell to her husband, her many children, and her friends, some of whom related afterward that "her sayings were as serious, religious, distinct, and affectionate as could well be expressed, drawing tears from the eyes of almost all present."

MRS. CLOYSE.

The third of this family of dignified gentlewomen seems to have had a keener sensibility than her sisters, or a frame less strong to endure the shocks prepared and inflicted by the malice of the enemy. Some of the incidents of her implication in the great calamity are almost too moving to be dwelt on, even in a remote time and country. Mrs. Cloyse drew ill-will upon herself at the outset by doing as her brother and sister Nurse did. They all absented themselves from the examinations in the church, and, when the interruptions of the services became too flagrant, from Sabbath worship; and they said they took that course because they disapproved of the permission given to the profanation of the place and the service. They were communicants, and persons of consideration, both in regard to character and position; and their quiet disapprobation of the proceedings of the ministers and their company of accusers subjected them to the full fury of clerical wrath and womanish spite. When the first examination of Mrs. Nurse took place, Mrs. Cloyse was of course overwhelmed with horror and grief. The next Sunday, however, was Sacrament Sunday; and she and her husband considered it their duty to attend the ordinance. The effort to Mrs. Cloyse was so great that when Mr. Parris gave out his text, "One of you is a devil. He spake of Judas Iscariot," etc., and when he opened his discourse with references in his special manner to the transactions of the week, the afflicted sister of the last victim could not endure the outrage. She left the meeting. There was a fresh wind, and the door slammed as she went out, fixing the attention of all present, just as Mr. Parris could have desired. She had not to wait long for the consequences. On the 4th of April she was apprehended with several others; and on the 11th her examination took place, the questions being framed to suit the evidence known to be forthcoming, and Mr. Parris being the secretary for the occasion. The witness in one case was asked whether she saw a company eating and drinking at Mr. Parris', and she replied, as expected, that she did. "What were they eating and drinking?" Of course, it was the Devil's sacrament; and Mr. Parris, by leading questions, brought out the testimony that about forty persons partook of that hell-sacrament, Mrs. Cloyse and Sarah Good being the two deacons! When accused of the usual practices of cruelty to these innocent suffering children, and to the ugly, hulking Indian slave, who pretended to show the marks of her teeth, Mrs. Cloyse gave some vent to her feelings. "When did I hurt thee?" "A great many times," said the Indian. "O, you are a grievous liar!" exclaimed she. But the wrath gave way under the soul-sickness which overcame her when charged with biting and pinching a black man, and throttling children, and serving their blood at the blasphemous supper. Her sisters in prison, her husband accused with her, and young girls —mere children—now manifesting a devilish cruelty to her, who had felt nothing but good-will to them—she could not sustain herself before the assembly whose eyes were upon her. She sank down, calling for water. She fainted on the floor, and some of the accusing children cried out, "Oh! her spirit has gone to prison to her sister Nurse!" From that examination she was herself carried to prison.

When she joined her sister Easty in the petition to the Court in the next summer, she certainly had no idea of escaping the gallows; but it does not appear that she was ever brought to trial. Mr. Parris certainly never relented; for we find him from time to time torturing the feelings of this and every other family whom he supposed to be anything but affectionate to him. Some of the incidents would be almost incredible to us if they were not recorded in the church and parish books in Mr. Parris' own distinct handwriting.

On the 14th of August, when the corpse of Rebecca Nurse was lying among the rocks on the Witches' Hill, and her two sisters were in irons in Boston jail (for Boston had now taken the affair out of the hands of the unaided Salem authorities), and his predecessor, Mr. Burroughs, was awaiting his execution, Mr. Parris invited his church members to remain after service to hear something that he had to say.

He had to point out to the vigilance of the church that Samuel Nurse, the son of Rebecca, and his wife, and Peter Cloyse and certain others, of late had failed to join the brethren at the Lord's table, and had, except Samuel Nurse, rarely appeared at ordinary worship. These outraged and mourning relatives of the accused sisters were decreed to be visited by certain pious representatives of the church, and the reason of their absence to be demanded. The minister, the two deacons, and a chief member were appointed to this fearful task. The report delivered in on the 31st of August was:

"Brother Tarbell proves sick, unmeet for discourse; Brother Cloyse hard to be found at home, being often with his wife in the prison at Ipswich for witchcraft; and Brother Samuel Nurse, and sometimes his wife, attends our public meeting, and he the sacrament, 11th of September, 1692: upon all which we chose to wait further." (Vol. ii. p. 486.)

This decision to pause was noted as the first token of the decline of the power of the ministers. Mr. Parris was sorely unwilling to yield even this much advantage to Satan—that is, to family affection and instinct of justice. But his position was further lowered by the departure from the parish of some of the most eminent members of its society. Mr. Cloyse never brought his family to the Village again, when his wife was once out of prison; and the name disappears from the history of Salem.

THE PROCTOR FAMILY.

We have sketched the life of one family out of many, and we will leave the rest for such of our readers as may choose to learn more. Some of the statements in the book before us disclose a whole family history in a few words; as the following in relation to John Proctor and his wife:

"The bitterness of the prosecutors against Proctor was so vehement that they not only arrested, and tried to destroy, his wife and all his family above the age of infancy, in Salem, but all her relatives in Lynn, many of whom were thrown into prison. The helpless children were left destitute, and the house swept of its provisions by the sheriff. Proctor's wife gave birth to a child about a fortnight after his execution. This indicates to what alone she owed her life. John Proctor had spoken so boldly against the proceedings, and all who had part in them, that it was felt to be necessary to put him out of the way." (Vol. ii. p. 312.)

The Rev. Mr. Noyes, the worthy coadjutor of Mr. Parris, refused to pray with Mr. Proctor before his death, unless he would confess; and the more danger there seemed to be of a revival of pity, humility, and reason, the more zealous waxed the wrath of the pious pastors against the Enemy of Souls. When, on the fearful 22d of September, Mr. Noyes stood looking at the execution, he exclaimed that it was a sad thing to see eight firebrands of hell hanging there! The spectacle was never seen again on Witches' Hill.

THE JACOBS FAMILY.

The Jacobs family was signalized by the confession of one of its members — Margaret, one of the "afflicted" girls. She brought her grandfather to the gallows, and suffered as much as a weak, ignorant, impressionable person under evil influences could suffer from doubt and remorse. But she married well seven years afterward — still feeling enough in regard to the past to refuse to be married by Mr. Noyes. She deserved such peace of mind as she obtained, for she retracted the confession of witchcraft which she had made, and went to prison. It was too late then to save her victims, Mr. Burroughs and her grandfather, but she obtained their full and free forgiveness. At that time this was the condition of the family:

"No account has come to us of the deportment of George Jacobs, Sr., at his execution. As he was remarkable in life for the firmness of his mind, so he probably was in death. He had made his will before the delusion arose. It is dated January 29, 1692, and shows that he, like Proctor, had a considerable estate. . . . . In his infirm old age he had been condemned to die for a crime of which he knew himself innocent, and which there is some reason to believe he did not think any one capable of committing. He regarded the whole thing as a wicked conspiracy and absurd fabrication. He had to end his long life upon a scaffold in a week from that day. His house was desolated, and his property sequestered. His only son, charged with the same crime, had eluded the sheriff — leaving his family, in the hurry of his flight, unprovided for — and was an exile in foreign lands. The crazy wife of that son was in prison and in chains, waiting trial on the same charge; her little children, including an unweaned infant, left in a deserted and destitute condition in the woods. The older children were scattered he knew not where, while one of them had completed the bitterness of his lot by becoming a confessor, upon being arrested with her mother as a witch. This granddaughter, Margaret, overwhelmed with fright and horror, bewildered by the statements of the accusers, and controlled probably by the arguments and arbitrary methods of address employed by her minister, Mr. Noyes—whose peculiar function in those proceedings seems to have been to drive persons accused to make confession—had been betrayed into that position, and became a confessor and accuser of others." (Vol. ii. p. 312.)

GILES AND MARTHA COREY.

The life and death of a prominent citizen, Giles Corey, should not be altogether passed over in a survey of such a community and such a time. He had land, and was called "Goodman Corey;" but he was unpopular from being too rough for even so young a state of society. He was once tried for the death of a man whom he had used roughly, but he was only fined. He had strifes and lawsuits with his neighbors; but he won three wives, and there was due affection between him and his children. He was eighty years old when the Witch Delusion broke out, and was living alone with his wife Martha—a devout woman who spent much of her time on her knees, praying against the snares of Satan, that is, the delusion about witchcraft. She spoke freely of the tricks of the children, the blindness of the magistrates, and the falling away of many from common sense and the word of God; and while her husband attended every public meeting, she stayed at home to pray. In his fanaticism he quarreled with her, and she was at once marked out for a victim, and one of the earliest. When visited by examiners, she smiled, and conversed with entire composure, declaring that she was no witch, and that "she did not think that there were any witches." By such sayings, and by the expressions of vexation that fell from her husband, and the fanaticism of two of her four sons-in-law, she was soon brought to extremity. But her husband was presently under accusation too; and much amazed he evidently was at his position. His wife was one of the eight " firebrands of hell" whom Mr. Noyes saw swung off on the 22d of September. "Martha Corey," said the record, " protesting her innocency, concluded her life with an eminent prayer on the scaffold." Her husband had been supposed certain to die in the same way; but he had chosen a different one. His anguish at his rash folly at the outset of the delusion excited the strongest desire to bear testimony on behalf of his wife and other innocent persons, and to give an emphatic blessing to the two sons-in-law who had been brave and faithful in his wife's cause. He executed a deed by which he presented his excellent children with his property in honor of their mother's memory; and, aware that if tried he would be condemned and executed, and his property forfeited, he resolved not to plead, and to submit to the consequence of standing mute. Old as he was, he endured it. He stood mute, and the court had, as the authorities believed, no alternative. He was pressed to death, as devoted husbands and fathers were, here and there, in the Middle Ages, when they chose to save their families from the consequences of attainders by dying untried. We will not sicken our readers with the details of the slow, cruel, and disgusting death. He bore it, only praying for heavier weights to shorten his agony. Such a death and such a testimony, and the execution of his wife two days later, weighed on every heart in the community; and no revival of old charges against the rough colonist had any effect in the presence of such an act as his last. He was long believed to haunt the places where he lived and died; and the attempt made by the ministers and one of their "afflicted" agents to impress the church and society with a vision which announced his damnation, was a complete failure. Cotton Mather showed that Ann Putnam had received a divine communication, proving Giles Corey a murderer; and Ann Putnam's father laid the facts before the judge; but it was too late now for visions, and for insinuations to the judges, and for clerical agitation to have any success. Brother Noyes hurried on a church meeting while Giles Corey was actually lying under the weights, to excommunicate him for witchcraft on the one hand, or suicide on the other; and the ordinance was passed. But it was of no avail against the rising tide of reason and sympathy. This was the last vision, and the last attempt to establish one in Salem, if not in the Province. It remained for Mr. Noyes, and the Mathers, and Mr. Parris, and every clergyman concerned, to endure the popular hatred and their own self-questioning for the rest of their days. The lay authorities were stricken with remorse and humbled with grief; but their share of the retribution was more endurable than that of the pastors who had proved so wolfish toward their flocks.

DECLINE OF THE DELUSION.

In the month of September, 1692, they believed themselves in the thick of "the fight between the Devil and the Lamb." Cotton Mather was nimble and triumphant on the Witches' Hill whenever there were "firebrands of hell" swinging there; and they all hoped to do much good work for the Lord yet, for they had lists of suspected persons in their pockets, who must be brought into the courts month by month, and carted off to the hill. One of the gayest and most complacent letters on the subject of this "fight" in the correspondence of Cotton Mather is dated on the 20th of September, 1692, within a month of the day when he was improving the occasion at the foot of the gallows where the former pastor, Rev. George Burroughs, and four others were hung. In the interval fifteen more received sentence of death; Giles Corey had died his fearful death the day before; and in two days after, Corey's widow and seven more were hanged. Mather, Noyes, and Parris had no idea that these eight would be the last. But so it was. Thus far, one only had escaped after being made sure of in the courts. The married daughter of a clergyman had been condemned, was reprieved by the Governor, and was at last discharged on the ground of the insufficiency of the evidence. Henceforth, after that fearful September day, no evidence was found sufficient. The accusers had grown too audacious in their selection of victims; their clerical patrons had become too openly determined to give no quarter. The Rev. Francis Dane signed memorials to the Legislature and the Courts on the 18th of October, against the prosecutions. He had reason to know something about them, for we hear of nine at least of his children, grandchildren, relatives, and servants who had been brought under accusation. He pointed out the snare by which the public mind, as well as the accused themselves, had been misled—the escape afforded to such as would confess. When one spoke out, others followed. When a reasonable explanation was afforded, ordinary people were only too thankful to seize upon it. Though the prisons were filled, and the courts occupied over and over again, there were no more horrors; the accused were all acquitted; and in the following May, Sir William Phipps discharged all the prisoners by proclamation. "Such a jail-delivery has never been known in New England," is the testimony handed down. The Governor was aware that the clergy, magistrates, and judges, hitherto active, were full of wrath at his course but public opinion now demanded a reversal of the administration of the last fearful year.

THE PHYSIO-PSYCHOLOGICAL CAUSES OF THE TROUBLE.

As to the striking feature of the case—the confessions of so large a proportion of the accused—Mr. Upham manifests the perplexity which we encounter in almost all narrators of similar scenes. In all countries and times in which trials for witchcraft have taken place, we find the historians dealing anxiously with the question—how it could happen that so many persons declared themselves guilty of an impossible offense, when the confession must seal their doom? The solution most commonly offered is one that may apply to a case here and there, but certainly can not be accepted as disposing of any large number. It is assumed that the victim preferred being killed at once to living on under suspicion, insult, and ill-will, under the imputation of having dealt with the Devil. Probable as this may be in the case of a stout-hearted, reasoning, forecasting person possessed of nerve to carry out a policy of suicide, it can never be believed of any considerable proportion of the ordinary run of old men and women charged with sorcery. The love of life and the horror of a cruel death at the hands of the mob or of the hangman are too strong to admit of a deliberate sacrifice so bold, on the part of terrified and distracted old people like the vast majority of the accused; while the few of a higher order, clearer in mind and stronger in nerve, would not be likely to effect their escape from an unhappy life by a lie of the utmost conceivable gravity. If, in the Salem case, life was saved by confession toward the last, it was for a special reason; and it seems to be a singular instance of such a mode of escape. Some other mode of explanation is needed; and the observations of modern inquiry supply it. There can be no doubt now that the sufferers under nervous disturbances, the subjects of abnormal condition, found themselves in possession of strange faculties, and thought themselves able to do new and wonderful things. When urged to explain how it was, they could only suppose, as so many of the Salem victims did, that it was by "some evil spirit;" and except where there was such an intervening agency as Mr. Parris' "circle," the only supposition was that the intercourse between the Evil Spirit and themselves was direct. It is impossible even now to witness the curious phenomena of somnambulism and catalepsy without a keen sense of how natural and even inevitable it was for similar subjects of the Middle Ages and in Puritan times to believe themselves ensnared by Satan, and actually endowed with his gifts, and to confess their calamity, as the only relief to their scared and miserable minds. This explanation seems not to have occurred to Mr. Upham; and, for want of it, he falls into great amazement at the elaborate artifice with which the sufferers invented their confessions, and adapted them to the state of mind of the authorities and the public. With the right key in his hand, he would have seen only what was simple and natural where he now bids us marvel at the pitch of artfulness and skill attained by poor wretches scared out of their natural wits.

The spectacle of the ruin that was left is very melancholy. Orphan children were dispersed; homes were shut up, and properties lost; and what the temper was in which these transactions left the churches and the village, and the society of the towns, the pastors and the flocks, the Lord's table, the social gathering, the justice hall, the market, and every place where men were wont to meet, we can conceive. It was evidently long before anything like a reasonable and genial temper returned to society in and about Salem. The acknowledgments of error made long after were half-hearted, and so were the expressions of grief and pity in regard to the intolerable woes of the victims. It is scarcely intelligible how the admissions on behalf of the wronged should have been so reluctant, and the sympathy with the devoted love of their nearest and dearest so cold. We must cite what Mr. Upham says in honor of these last, for such solace is needed:

"While, in the course of our story, we have witnessed some shocking instances of the violation of the most sacred affections and obligations of life, in husbands and wives, parents and children, testifying against each other, and exerting themselves for mutual destruction, we must not overlook the many instances in which filial, parental, and fraternal fidelity and love have shone conspicuously. It was dangerous to befriend an accused person. Proctor stood by his wife to protect her, and it cost him his life. Children protested against the treatment of their parents, and they were all thrown into prison. Daniel Andrew, a citizen of high standing, who had been deputy to the General Court, asserted, in the boldest language, his belief of Rebecca Nurse's innocence; and he had to fly the country to save his life. Many devoted sons and daughters clung to their parents, visited them in prison in defiance of a blood-thirsty mob; kept by their side on the way to execution; expressed their love, sympathy, and reverence to the last; and, by brave and perilous enterprise, got possession of their remains, and bore them back under the cover of midnight to their own thresholds, and to graves kept consecrated by their prayers and tears. One noble young man is said to have effected his mother's escape from the jail, and secreted her in the woods until after the delusion had passed away, provided food and clothing for her, erected a wigwam for her shelter, and surrounded her with every comfrot her situation would admit of. The poor creature must, however, have endured a great amount of suffering; for one of her larger limbs was fractured in the all but desperate attempt to rescue her from the prison walls." (Vol. ii. p. 348.)

The act of reversal of attainder, passed early in the next century, tells us that "some of the principal accusers and witnesses in those dark and severe prosecutions have since discovered themselves to be persons of profligate and vicious conversation;" and on no other authority we are assured that, "not without spot before, they became afterward abandoned to open vice." This was doubtless true of some; but of many it was not; and of this we shall have a word to say presently.

THE LAST OF PARRIS.

Mr. Parris' parsonage soon went to ruin, as did some of the dwellings of the "afflicted" children, who learned and practiced certain things in his house which he afterward pronounced to be arts of Satan, and declared to have been pursued without his knowledge and with the cognizance of only his servants (John and Tituba, the Indian and the negress). Barn, and well, and garden disappeared in a sorry tract of rough ground, and the dwelling became a mere handful of broken bricks. The narrative of the pastor's struggles and devices to retain his pulpit is very interesting; but they are not related to our object here; and all we need say is, that three sons and sons-in-law of Mrs. Nurse measured their strength against his, and, without having said an intemperate or superfluous word, or swerved from the strictest rules of congregational action, sent him out of the parish. He finally opined that "evil angels" had been permitted to tempt him and his coadjutors on either hand; he admitted that some mistakes had been made; and, said he, "I do humbly own this day, before the Lord and his people, that God has been righteously spitting in my face; and I desire to lie low under all this reproach," etc.; but the remonstrants could not again sit under his ministry, and his brethren in the Province did not pretend to exculpate him altogether. He buried his wife—against whom no record remains—and departed with his children, the eldest of whom, the playfellow of the "afflicted" children, he had sent away before she had taken harm in the "circle." He drifted from one small outlying congregation to another, neglected and poor, restless and untamed, though mortified, till he died in 1720. Mr. Noyes died somewhat earlier. He is believed not to have undergone much change, as to either his views or his temper. He was a kind-hearted and amiable man when nothing came in the way; but he could hold no terms with Satan; and in this he insisted to the last that he was right.

Cotton Mather was the survivor of the other two. He died in 1728; and he never was happy again after that last batch of executions. He trusted to his merits, and the genius he exhibited under that onslaught of Satan, to raise him to the highest post of clerical power in the Province, and to make him—what he desired above all else—President of Harvard University. Mr. Upham presents us with a remarkable meditation written by the unhappy man, so simple and ingenious that it is scarcely possible to read it gravely; but the reader is not the less sensible of his misery. The argument is a sort of remonstrance with God on the recompense his services have met with. He has been appointed to serve the world, and the world does not regard him; the negroes, and (who could believe it?) the negroes are named Cotton Mather in contempt of him; the wise and the unwise despise him; in every company he is avoided and left alone; the female sex, and they speak basely of him; his relatives, and they are such monsters that he may truly say, "I am a brother to dragons;" the Government, and it heaps indignities upon him; the University, and if he were a blockhead, it could not treat him worse than it does. He is to serve all whom he can aid, and nobody ever does anything for him; he is to serve all to whom he can be a helpful and happy minister, and yet he is the most afflicted minister in the country; and many consider his afflictions to be so many miscarriages, and his sufferings in proportion to his sins. There was no popularity or power for him from the hour when he stood to see his brother Burroughs put to death on the Hill. He seems never to have got over his surprise at his own failures; but he sank into deeper mortification and a more childish peevishness to the end.

"ONE OF THE AFFLICTED"—HER CONFESSION.

Of only one of the class of express accusers—of the "afflicted"—will we speak; but not because she was the only one reclaimed. One bewildered child we have described as remorseful, and brave in her remorse; and others married as they would hardly have done if they had been among the "profligate." Ann Putnam's case remains the most prominent, and the most pathetic. She was twelve years old when the "circle" at Mr. Parris' was formed. She had no check from her parents, but much countenance and encouragement from her morbidly-disposed mother. She has the bad distinction of having been the last of the witnesses to declare a "vision" against a suspected person; but, on the other hand, she has the honor, such as it is, of having striven to humble herself before the memory of her victims. When she was nineteen her father died, and her mother followed within a fortnight, leaving the poor girl, in bad health and with scanty means, to take care of a family of children so large that there were eight, if not more, dependent on her. No doubt she was aided, and she did what she could; but she died worn out at the age of thirty-six. Ten years before that date she made her peace with the Church and society by offering a public confession in the meeting-house. In order to show what it was that the accusers did admit, we must make room for Ann Putnam's confession:

"'I desire to be humbled before God for that sad and humbling providence that befell my father's family in the year about '92; that I, then being in my childhood, should, by such a providence of God, be made the instrument for the accusing of several persons of a grievous crime, whereby their lives were taken away from them, whom now I have just grounds and good reason to believe they were innocent persons; and that it was a great delusion of Satan that deceived me in that sad time, whereby I justly fear that I have been instrumental with others, though ignorantly and unwittingly, to bring upon myself and this land the guilt of innocent blood; though what was said or done by me against any person I can truly and uprightly say, before God and man, I did it not out of any anger, malice, or ill-will to any person, for I had no such thing against one of them; but what I did was ignorantly, being deluded by Satan. And particularly, as I was a chief instrument of accusing Goodwife Nurse and her two sisters, I desire to lie in the dust, and to be humbled for it, in that I was a cause, with others, of so sad a calamity to them and their families; for which cause I desire to lie in the dust, and earnestly beg forgiveness of God, and from all those unto whom I have given just cause of sorrow and offense, whose relations were taken away or accused. (Signed) Ann Putnam.'

"This confession was read before the congregation, together with her relation, August 25, 1706; and she acknowledged it.

"J. GREEN, *Pastor*." (Vol. ii. p. 510.)

THE TRANSITION.

The most agreeable picture ever afforded by this remarkable community is that which our eyes rest on at the close of the story. One of the church members had refused to help to send Mr. Parris away, on the ground that the village had had four pastors, and had gone through worse strifes with every one; but he saw a change of scene on the advent of the fifth. The Rev. Joseph Green was precisely the man for the place and occasion. He was young—only two-and-twenty—and full of hope and cheerfulness, while sobered by the trials of the time. He had a wife and infants, and some private property, so that he could at once plant down a happy home among his people, without any injurious dependence on them. While exemplary in clerical duty, he encouraged an opposite tone of mind to that which had prevailed—put all the devils out of sight, promoted pigeon-shooting and fishing, and headed the young men in looking after hostile Indians. Instead of being jealous at the uprising of new churches, he went to lay the foundations, and invited the new brethren to his home. He promoted the claims of the sufferers impoverished by the recent social convulsion; he desired to bury not only delusions, but ill offices in silence; and by his hospitality he infused a cheerful social spirit into his stricken people. The very business of "seating" the congregation was so managed under his ministry as that members of the sinning and suffering families—members not in too direct an antagonism—were brought together for prayer, singing, and Sabbath-greeting, forgiving and forgetting as far as possible. Thus did this excellent pastor create a new scene of peace and good-will, which grew brighter for eighteen years, when he died at the age of forty. At the earliest moment that was prudent, he induced his church to cancel the excommunication of Rebecca Nurse and Giles Corey. It was ten years more before the hard and haughty mother church in Salem would do its part; but Mr. Green had the satisfaction of seeing that record also cleansed of its foul stains three years before his death. Judge Sewall had before made his penitential acknowledgment of proud error in full assembly, and had resumed his seat on the bench amid the forgiveness and respect of society; Chief Justice Stoughton had retired from the courts in obstinate rage at his conflicts with Satan having been cut short; the physicians hoped they should have no more patients "under the evil hand," to make them look foolish and feel helpless; and the Tragedy was over. There were doubtless secret tears and groans, horrors of shame and remorse by night and by day, and indignant removal of the bones of the murdered from outcast graves; and abstraction of painful pages from books of record, and much stifling of any conversation which could grow into tradition. The Tragedy was, no doubt, the central interest of society, families, and individuals throughout the Province for the life of one generation. Then, as silence had been kept in the homes as well as at church and market, the next generation entered upon life almost unconscious of the ghastly distinction which would attach in history to Massachusetts in general, and Salem in particular, as the scene of the Delusion and the Tragedy which showed the New World to be in essentials no wiser than the Old.

How effectually the story of that year 1692 was buried in silence is shown by a remark of Mr. Upham's—that it has been too common for the Witch Tragedy to be made a jest of, or at least to be spoken of with levity. We can have no doubt that his labors have put an end to this. It is inconceivable that there can ever again be a joke heard on the subject of Witchcraft in Salem. But this remark of our author brings us at once home to our own country, time, and experience. It suggests the question whether the lesson afforded by this singular perfect piece of history is more or less appropriate to our own day and generation.

THE FETISH THEORY THEN AND NOW.

We have already observed that at the date of these events, the only possible explanation of the phenomena presented was the fetish solution which had in all ages been recurred to as a matter of course. In heathen times it was god, goddess, or nymph who gave knowledge, or power, or gifts of healing, or of prophecy, to men. In Christian times it was angel, or devil, or spirit of the dead; and this conception was in full force over all Christendom when the Puritan emigrants settled in New England. The celebrated sermon of the Rev. Mr. Lawson, in the work before us, discloses the elaborate doctrine held by the class of men who were supposed to know best in regard to the powers given by Satan to his agents, and the evils with which he afflicted his victims; and there was not only no reason why the pastor's hearers should question his interpretations, but no possibility that they should supply any of a different kind. The accused themselves, while unable to admit or conceive that they were themselves inspired by Satan, could propose no explanation but that the acts were done by "some bad spirit." And such has been the fetish tendency to this hour, through all the advance that has been made in science, and in the arts of observation and of reasoning. The fetish tendency—that of ascribing one's own consciousness to external objects, as when the dog takes a watch to be alive because it ticks, and when the savage thinks his god is angry because it thunders, and when the Puritan catechumen cries out in hysteria that Satan has set a witch to strangle her—that constant tendency to explain everything by the facts, the feelings, and the experience of the individual's own nature, is no nearer dying out now than at the time of the Salem Tragedy; and hence, in part, the seriousness and the instructiveness of this story to the present generation. Ours is the generation which has seen the spread of Spiritualism in Europe and America, a phenomenon which deprives us of all right to treat the Salem Tragedy as a jest, or to adopt a tone of superiority in compassion for the agents in that dismal drama. There are hundreds, even several thousands, of lunatics in the asylums of the United States, and not a few in our own country, who have been lodged there by the pursuit of intercourse with spirits; in other words, by ascribing to living but invisible external agents movements of their own minds. Mr. Parris remarked, in 1692, that of old, witches were only ignorant old women; whereas, in his day, they had come to be persons of knowledge, holiness, and devotion who had been drawn into that damnation; and in our day, we hear remarks on the superior refinement of spirit-intercourses, in comparison with the witch doings at Salem; but the cases are all essentially the same. In all, some peculiar and inexplicable appearances occur, and are, as a matter of course, when their reality can not be denied, ascribed to spiritual agency. We may believe that we could never act as the citizens of Salem acted in their superstition and their fear; and this may be true; but the course of speculation is, in "spiritual circles," very much the same as in Mr. Parris' parlor.

And how much less excuse there is for our generation than for his! We are very far yet from being able to explain the well-known and indisputable facts which occur from time to time, in all countries where men abide and can give an account of themselves; such facts as the phenomena of natural somnambulism, of double consciousness, of suspended sensation while consciousness is awake, and the converse—of a wide range of intellectual and instinctive operations bearing the character of marvels to such as can not wait for the solution. We are still far from being able to explain such mysteries, in the only true sense of the word *explaining*—that is, being able to refer the facts to the natural cause to which they belong; but we have an incalculable advantage over the people of former centuries in knowing that for all proved facts there is a natural cause; that every cause to which proved facts within our cognizance are related is destined to become known to us; and that, in the present case, we have learned in what direction to search for it, and have set out on the quest. None of us can offer even the remotest conjecture as to what the law of the common action of what we call mind and body may be. If we could, the discovery would have been already made. But, instead of necessarily assuming, as the Salem people did, that what they witnessed was the operation of spiritual upon human beings, we have, as our field of observation and study, a region undreamed of by them—the brain as an organized part of the human frame, and the nervous system, implicating more facts, more secrets, and more marvels than our forefathers attributed to the whole body.

THE VIEWS OF MODERN INVESTIGATORS.

It is very striking to hear the modern lectures on physiological subjects delivered in every capital in Europe, and to compare the calm and easy manner in which the most astonishing and the most infernal phenomena are described and discussed, with the horror and dismay that the same facts would have created if disclosed by divines in churches three centuries ago. Dr. Maudsley, in his recent work on " The Physiology and Pathology of Mind," and other physicians occupied in his line of practice, lead us through the lunatic asylums of every country, pointing out as ordinary or extraordinary incidents the same "afflictions" of children and other morbid persons which we read of, one after another, in the Salem story. It is a matter of course with such practitioners and authors to anticipate such phenomena when they have detected the morbid conditions which generate them. Mr. Upham himself is evidently very far indeed from understanding or suspecting how much light is thrown on the darkest part of his subject by physiological researches carried on to the hour when he laid down his pen. His view is confined almost exclusively to the theory of fraud and falsehood, as affording the true key. It is not probable that anybody disputes or doubts the existence of guilt and folly in many or all of the agents concerned. There was an antecedent probability of both in regard to Mr. Parris' slaves, and to such of the young children as they most influenced; and that kind of infection is apt to spread. Moreover, experience shows us that the special excitement of that nervous condition induces moral vagaries at least as powerfully as mental delusions. In the state of temper existing among the inhabitants of the Village when the mischievous club of girls was formed at the pastor's house, it was inevitable that, if magic was entered upon at all, it would be malignant magic. Whatever Mr. Upham has said in illustration of that aspect of the case his readers will readily agree to. But there is a good deal more, even of the imperfect notices that remain after the abstraction and destruction of the records in the shame and anguish that ensued, which we, in our new dawn of science, can perceive to be an affair of the bodily organization. We are, therefore, obliged to him for rescuing this tremendous chapter of history from oblivion, and for the security in which he has placed the materials of evidence. In another generation the science of the human frame may have advanced far enough to elucidate some of the Salem mysteries, together with some obscure facts in all countries, which can not be denied, while as yet they can not be understood. When that time comes, a fearful weight of imputation will be removed from the name and fame of many agents and sufferers who have been the subjects of strange maladies and strange faculties, in all times and countries. As we are now taught the new discoveries of the several nerve-centers, and the powers which are appropriated to them; and when we observe what a severance may exist between the so-called organ of any sense or faculty and the operation of the sense or faculty; and how infallibly ideas and emotion may be generated, and even beliefs created in minds sane and insane, by certain manipulations of the nerves and brain, we see how innocently this phenomenon may be presented in natural somnambulism. Sleep-walkers have been known in many countries, and treated of in medical records by their physicians, who could not only walk, and perform all ordinary acts in the dark as well as in the light, but who went on writing or reading without interruption though an opaque substance—a book or a slate—was interposed, and would dot the *i's* and cross the *t's* with unconscious correctness without any use of their eyes. There is a wide field of inquiry open in this direction, now that the study of the nervous system has been begun, however minute is the advance as yet.

IMPORTANCE OF THE SUBJECT.

It is needless to dwell on the objection made to the rising hopefulness in regard to the study of Man, and the mysteries of his nature. Between the multitude who have still no notion of any alternative supposition to that of possession or inspiration by spirits, or, at least, intercourse with such beings, and others who fear "Materialism" if too close an attention is paid to the interaction of the mind and the nerves, and those who always shrink from new notions in matters so interesting, and those who fear that religion may be implicated in any slight shown to angel or devil, and those who will not see or hear any evidence whatever which lies in a direction opposite to their prejudices, we are not likely to get on too fast. But neither can the injury lapse under neglect. The spectacle presented now is of the same three sorts of people that appear in all satires, in all literatures, since the pursuit of truth in any mode or direction became a recognized object anywhere and under any conditions. Leaving out of view the multitude who are irrelevant to the case, from having no knowledge, and being therefore incapable of an opinion, there is the large company of the superficial and light-minded, who are always injuring the honor and beauty of truth by the levity, the impertinence, the absurdity of the enthusiasm they pretend, and the nonsense they talk about "some new thing." No period of society has been more familiar with that class and its mischief-making than our own. There is the other large class of the cotemporaries of any discovery or special advance, who, when they can absent themselves from the scene no longer, look and listen, and bend all their efforts to hold their ground of life-long opinion, usually succeeding so far as to escape any direct admission that more is known than when they were born. These are no ultimate hindrance. When Harvey died, no physician in Europe above the age of forty believed in the circulation of the blood; but the truth was perfectly safe; and so it will be with the case of the psychological relations of the nervous system when the present course of investigation has sustained a clearer verification and further advance. On this point we have the sayings of two truth-seekers, wise in quality of intellect, impartial and dispassionate in temper, and fearless in the pursuit of their aims. The late Prince Consort is vividly remembered for the characteristic saying which spread rapidly over the country, that he could not understand the conduct of the medical profession in England in leaving the phenomena of mesmerism to the observation of unqualified persons, instead of undertaking an inquiry which was certainly their proper business, in proportion as they professed to pursue *science*. The other authority we refer to is the late Mr. Hallam. A letter of his lies before us from which we quote a passage, familiar in its substance, doubtless, to his personal friends, to whom he always avowed the view which it presents, and well worthy of note to such readers as may not be aware of the observation and thought he devoted to the phenomena of mesmerism during the last quarter-century of his long life. "It appears to me probable that the various phenomena of mesmerism, together with others, independent of mesmerism properly so called, which have lately [the date is 1844] been brought to light, are fragments of some general law of nature which we are not yet able to deduce from them, merely because they are destitute of visible connection—the links being hitherto wanting which are to display the entire harmony of effects proceeding from a single cause."

[Persons curious to know what has been developed in this class of studies may find the same in a work published at this office, entitled THE LIBRARY OF MESMERISM AND PSYCHOLOGY—comprising the Philosophy of Mesmerism, Clairvoyance, and Mental Electricity; Fascination, or the Power of Charming; The Macrocosm, or the World of Sense; Electrical Psychology, or the Doctrine of Impressions; The Science of the Soul, treated Physiologically and Philosophically. Complete in one illustrated volume. Price, $4.]

What room is there not for hopefulness when we compare such an observation as this with Mr. Parris' dogmatical exposition of Satan's dealings with men! or when we contrast the calm and cheerful tone of the philosopher with the stubborn wrath of Chief Justice Stoughton, and with the penitential laments of Judge Sewall! We might contrast it also with the wild exultation of those of the Spiritualists of our own day who can form no conception of the modesty and patience requisite for the sincere search for truth, and who, once finding themselves surrounded by facts and appearances new and strange, assume that they have discovered a bridge over the bottomless "gulf beyond which lies the spirit-land," and wander henceforth in a fools' paradise, despising and pitying all who are less rash, ignorant, and presumptuous than themselves. It is this company of fanatics—the first of the three classes we spoke of—which is partly answerable for the backwardness of the second; but the blame does not rest exclusively in one quarter. There is an indolence in the medical class which is the commonest reproach against them in every age of scientific activity, and which has recently been heroically avowed and denounced in a public address by no less a member of the profession than Sir Thomas Watson.* There is a conservative reluctance to change of view or of procedure. There is also a lack of moral courage, by no means surprising in an order of men whose lives are spent in charming away troubles, and easing pains and cares, and "making things pleasant"—by no means surprising, we admit, but exceedingly unfavorable to the acknowledgment of phenomena that are strange and facts that are unintelligible.

This brings us to the third class—the very small number of persons who are, in the matter of human progress, the salt of the earth; the few who can endure to see without understanding, to hear without immediately believing or disbelieving, to learn what they can, without any consideration of what figure they themselves shall make in the transaction; and even to be unable to reconcile the new phenomena with their own prior experience or conceptions. There is no need to describe how rare this class must necessarily be, for every one who has eyes sees how near the passions and the prejudices of the human being lie to each other. These are the few who unite the two great virtues

---

* Address on the Present State of Therapeutics. Delivered at the opening meeting of the Clinical Society of London, January 10, 1868. By Sir Thomas Watson, Bart., M.D.

of earnestly studying the facts, and keeping their temper, composure, and cheerfulness through whatever perplexity their inquiry may involve. It is remarkable that while the world is echoing all round and incessantly with the praise of the life of the man spent in following truth wherever it may lead, the world is always resounding also with the angry passions of men who resent all opinions which are not their own, and denounce with fury or with malice any countenance given to mere proposals to inquire in certain directions which they think proper to reprobate. Not only was it horrible blasphemy in Galileo to think as he did of the motion of the earth, but in his friends to look through his glass at the stars.

This Salem story is indeed shocking in every view—to our pride as rational beings, to our sympathy as human beings, to our faith as Christians, to our complacency as children of the Reformation. It is so shocking that some of us may regret that the details have been revived with such an abundance of evidence. But this is no matter of regret, but rather of congratulation, if we have not outgrown the need of admonition from the past. How does that consideration stand?

At the end of nearly three centuries we find ourselves relieved of a heavy burden of fear and care about the perpetual and unbounded malice of Satan and his agents. Witchcraft has ceased to be one of the gravest curses of the human lot. We have parted with one after another of the fetish or conjectural persuasions about our relations with the world of spirit or mind, regarded as in direct opposition to the world of matter. By a succession of discoveries we have been led to an essentially different view of life and thought from any dreamed of before the new birth of science; and at this day, and in our own metropolis, we have Sir Henry Holland telling us how certain treatment of this or that department of the nervous system will generate this or that state of belief and experience, as well as sensation. We have Dr. Carpenter disclosing facts of incalculable significance about brain-action without consciousness, and other vital mysteries. We have Dr. Maudsley showing, in the cells of the lunatic asylum, not only the very realm of Satan, as our fathers would have thought, but the discovery that it is not Satan, after all, that makes the havoc, but our own ignorance which has seduced us into a blasphemous superstition, instead of inciting us to the study of ourselves. And these are not all our teachers. Amid the conflict of phenomena of the hu-

IMPORTANCE OF THE SUBJECT.

man mind and body, we have arrived now at the express controversy of Psychology against Physiology. Beyond the mere statement of the fact we have scarcely advanced a step. The first can not be, with any accuracy, called a science at all, and the other is in little more than a rudimentary state; but it is no small gain to have arrived at some conception of the nature of the problem set before us, and at some liberty of hypothesis as to its conditions. In brief, and in the plainest terms, while there is still a multitude deluding and disporting itself with a false hypothesis about certain mysteries of the human mind, and claiming to have explained the marvels of Spiritualism by making an objective world of their own subjective experience, the scientific physiologists [those especially who are true phrenologists] are proceeding, by observation and experiment, to penetrate more and more secrets of our intellectual and moral life.

THE PLANCHETTE MYSTERY.

WHAT PLANCHETTE IS AND DOES.

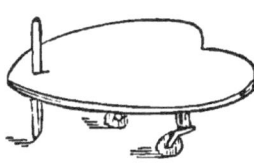

THE PLANCHETTE.

THIS little gyrating tripod is proving itself to be something more than a nine days' wonder. It is finding its way into thousands of families in all parts of the land. Lawyers, physicians, politicians, philosophers, and even clergymen, have watched eagerly its strange antics, and listened with rapt attention to its mystic oracles. Mrs. Jones demands of it where Jones spends his evenings; the inquisitive of both sexes are soliciting it to "tell their fortunes;" speculators are invoking its aid in making sharp bargains, and it is said that even sagacious brokers in Wall Street are often found listening to its vaticinations as to the price of stocks on a given future day. To all kinds of inquiries answers are given, intelligible at least, if not always true. A wonderful jumble of mental and moral possibilities is this little piece of dead matter, now giving utterance to childish drivel, now bandying jokes and badinage, now stirring the conscience by unexceptionably Christian admonitions, and now uttering the baldest infidelity or the most shocking profanity; and often discoursing gravely on science, philosophy, or theology. It is true that Planchette seldom assumes this variety of theme and diction under the hands of the same individual, but, in general, manifests a peculiar facility of adapting its discourse to the character of its associates. Reader, with your sanction, we will seek a little further acquaintance with this new wonder.

The word "Planchette" is French, and simply signifies a *little board*. It is usually made in the shape of a heart, about seven inches long and six inches wide at the widest part, but we suppose that any other shape and convenient size would answer as well. Under the two corners of the widest end are fixed two little castors or pantograph wheels, admitting of easy motion in all horizontal directions; and in a hole, pierced through the narrow end, is fixed, upright, a lead pencil, which forms the third foot of the tripod. If this little instrument be placed upon a sheet of printing paper, and the fingers of one or more persons be laid lightly upon it, after quietly waiting a short time for the connection or *rapport* to become established, the board, if conditions are favorable, will begin to move, carrying the fingers with it. It will move for about one person in every three or four; and sometimes it will move with the hands of two or three persons in contact with it, when it will not move for either one of the persons singly. At the first trial, from a few seconds to twenty minutes may be required to establish the motion; but at subsequent trials it will move almost immediately. The first movements are usually indefinite or in circles but as soon as some control of the motion is established, it will begin to write—at first, perhaps, in mere monosyllables, "Yes," and "No," in answer to leading questions, but afterward freely writing whole sentences, and even pages.

For me alone, the instrument will not move; for myself and wife it moves slightly, but its writing is mostly in monosyllables. With my daughter's hands upon it, it writes more freely, frequently giving, correctly, the names of persons present whom she may not know, and also the names of their friends, living or dead, with other and similar tests. Its conversations with her are grave or gay, much according to the state of her own mind at the time; and when frivolous questions are asked, it almost always returns answers either frivolous or, I am sorry to say it, a trifle wicked. For example, she on one occasion said to it: "Planchette, where did you get your education?" To her horror, it instantly wrote: "In h—l," without, however, being so fastidious as to omit the letters of the word here left out. On another occasion, after receiving from it responses to some trival questions, she said to it: "Planchette, now write something of your own accord without our prompting." But instead of writing words and sentences as was expected, it immediately traced out the rude figure of a man, such as school children sometimes make upon their slates. After finishing the outlines—face, neck, arms, legs, etc., it swung around and brought the point of the pencil to the proper position for the eye, which it carefully marked in, and then proceeded to pencil out the hair. On finishing this operation, it wrote under the figure the name of a young man concerning whom my daughter's companions are in the habit of teasing her.

My wife once said to it: "Planchette, write the name of the article I am thinking of." She was thinking of a finger ring, on which her eye had rested a moment before. The operator, of course, knew nothing of this, and my wife expected either that the experiment would fail, or else that the letters R-i-n-g would be traced. But instead of that, the instrument moved, very slowly, and, as it were, deliberately, and traced an apparently *exact circle* on the paper, of about the size of the finger ring she had in her mind. "Will you try that over again?" said she, when a similar circle was traced, in a similar manner, but more promptly. During this experiment, one of my wife's hands, in addition to my daughter's, was resting lightly upon the board; but if the moving force had been supplied by her, either consciously or unconsciously, the motion would evidently have taken the direction of her thought, which was that of writing the letters of the word, instead of a direction unthought of.

While Planchette, in her intercourse with me, has failed to distinguish herself either as a preacher or a philosopher, I regret to say that she has not proved herself a much more successful prophet. While the recent contest for the United States Senatorship from the State of New York was pending, I said to my little oracular friend: "Planchette, will you give me a test?" "Yes." "Do you know who will be the next U. S. Senator from this State?" "Yes." "Please write the name of the person who will be chosen." "*Mr. Sutton*," was written. Said I, "I have not the pleasure of knowing that gentleman; please tell me where he resides." *Ans.* "In Washington."

I do not relate this to disturb the happy dreams of the Hon. Reuben E. Fenton by suggesting any dire contingencies that may yet happen to mar the prospect before him. In justice to my little friend, however, I must not omit to state that in respect to questions as to the kind of weather we shall have on the morrow? will such person go, or such a one come? or shall I see, or do this, that, or the other thing? its responses have been generally correct.

To rush to a conclusion respecting the *rationale* of so mysterious a phenomenon, under the sole guidance of an experience which has been so limited as my own, would betray an amount of egoism and heedlessness with which I am unwilling to be chargeable; and my readers will now be introduced to some experiences of others.

A friend of mine, Mr. C., residing in Jersey City, with whom I have almost daily intercourse, and whose testimony is entirely trustworthy, relates the following:

Some five or six months ago he purchased a Planchette, brought it home, and placed it in the hands of Mrs. B., a widow, who was then visiting his family. Mrs. B. had never tried or witnessed any experiments with Planchette, and was incredulous as to her power to evoke any movements from it. She, however, placed her hands upon it, as directed, and to her surprise it soon began to move, and wrote for its first words: "Take care!" "Of what must I take care?" she inquired. "Of your money." "Where?" "In Kentucky."

My friend states that Mrs. B.'s husband had died in Albany about two years previous, bequeathing to her ten thousand dollars, which sum she had loaned to a gentleman in Louisville, Ky., to invest in the drug business, on condition that she and he were to share the profits; and up to this time the thought had not occurred to her that her money was not perfectly safe. At this point she inquired: "Who is this that is giving this caution?" "B—— W——." (The name of a friend of hers who had died at Cairo, Ill., some six years before.) Mrs. B. "Why! is my money in jeopardy?" Planchette. "Yes, and needs prompt attention." My friend C. here asked: "Ought she to go to Kentucky and attend to the matter?" "Yes."

So strange and unexpected was this whole communication, and so independent of the suggestions of her own mind, that she was not a little impressed by it, and thought it would at least be safe for her to make a journey to Louisville and ascertain if the facts were as represented. But she had at the time no ready money to pay her traveling expenses, and not knowing how she could get the money, she asked: "When shall I be able to go?" "In two weeks from to-day," was the reply.

She thought over the matter, and the next day applied to a friend of hers, a Mr. W., in Nassau Street, who promised to lend her the money by the next Tuesday or Wednesday. (It was on Thursday that the interview with Planchette occurred.) She came home and remarked to my friend: "Well, Planchette has told one lie, anyhow; it said I would start for Louisville *two weeks* from that day. Mr. W. is going to lend me the money, and I shall start by *next* Thursday, only *one* week from that time."

But on the next Tuesday morning she received a note from Mr. W. expressing regret that circumstances had occurred which would render it impossible for him to let her have the money. She immediately sought, and soon found, another person by whom she was promised the money still in time to enable her to start a couple of days before the expiration of the two weeks—thus still, as she supposed, enabling her to prove Planchette to be wrong in at least that particular. But from circumstances unnecessary to detail, the money did not come until Wednesday, the day before the expiration of the two weeks. She then prepared herself to start the next *morning;* but through a blunder of the expressman in carrying her trunk to the wrong depot, she was detained till the five o'clock P.M. train, when she started, just two weeks, *to the hour*, from the time the prediction was given.

Arriving in Louisville, she learned that her friend had become involved in consequence of having made a number of bad sales for large amounts, and had actually gone into bankruptcy—reserving, however, for the security of her debt, a number of lots of ground, which his creditors were trying to get hold of. She thus arrived not a moment too soon to save herself, which she will probably do, in good part, at least, if not wholly—though the affair is still unsettled.

Since this article was commenced, the following fact has been furnished me from a reliable source. It is offered not only for the test which it involves, but also to illustrate the remarkable faculty which Planchette sometimes manifests, of calling things by their right names. A lady well known to the community, but whose name I have not permission to disclose, recently received from Planchette, writing under her own hands, a communication so remarkable that she was induced to ask for the name of the intelligence that wrote it. In answer to her request, the name of the late Col. Baker, who gallantly fell at Ball's Bluff, was given, in a perfect *fac-simile* of his handwriting. She said to him: "For a further test, will you be kind enough to tell me where I last saw you?" She expected him to mention the place and occasion of their last interview when she had invited him to her house to tea; but Planchette wrote: "*In the hall of thieves.*" "In the hall of thieves," said the lady; "what on earth can be the meaning of that? O! I remember that after he was killed, his body was brought on here and laid in the City Hall, and there I saw him."

THE PRESS ON PLANCHETTE.

In Planchette, public journalists and pamphleteers seem to have caught the "What is it?" in a new shape, and great has been the expenditure of printer's ink in the way of narratives, queries, and speculations upon the subject. There are now lying before me the following publications and articles, in which the Planchette phenomena are noticed and discussed,—from which we propose to cull and condense such statements of fact as appear to possess most intrinsic interest, and promise most aid in the solution of the mysteries. Afterward we shall discuss the different theories of these writers, and also some other theories that have been propounded.

"PLANCHETTE'S DIARY," edited by Kate Field, is an entertaining pamphlet, consisting of details in the author's experience, with little or no speculation as to the origin or laws of the phenomena. The author herself was the principal medium of the communications, but she occasionally introduces experiences of others. The pamphlet serves to put one on familiar and companionable terms with the invisible source of intelligence, whatever that may be, illustrating the leading peculiarities of the phenomena, giving some tests of an outside directing influence more or less striking, and candidly recording the failures of test answers which were mixed up with the successes. We extract two or three specimens:

"May 26th—Evening. Our trio was reinforced by Mr. B., a clever young lawyer, who regarded Planchette with no favorable eye — had no faith whatever in 'Spiritualism,' and maintained that for his part he thought it quite as sensible, if not more so, to attribute unknown phenomena to white rabbits as to spirits. . . . Planchette addressed herself to Mr. B. thus:

'You do not think that I am a spirit. I tell you that I am. If I am not an intelligence, in the name of common sense what am I? If you fancy I am white rabbits, then all I have to say is, that white rabbits are a deal cleverer than they have the credit of being among natural historians.'

Later, doubt was thrown upon the possibility of getting mental questions answered, and Planchette retorted:

'Do you fancy for one moment that I don't know the workings of your brain? That is not the difficulty. It is the impossibility—almost —of making two diametrically opposed magnetisms unite.'

After this rebuke, Mr. B. asked a mental question, and received the following answer:

'I am impelled to say that if you will persevere in these investigations, you may be placed *en rapport* with your wife, who would undoubtedly communicate with you. If you have any faith in the immortality of the soul, you can have no doubt of the possibility of spiritual influences being brought to bear upon mortals. It is no new thing. Ever since the world began, this power has been exerted in one way or another; and if you pretend to put any faith in the Bible, you surely must credit the possibility of establishing this subtile connection between man and so-called angels.'

This communication was glibly written until within eleven words of the conclusion, when Planchette stopped, and I asked if she had finished.

'No,' she replied.

'Then why don't you go on?' I continued. '*I* can write faster than this.'

Planchette grew exceeding wroth at this, and dashed off an answer:

'Because, my good gracious! you are not obliged to express yourself through another's brain.'

I took it for granted that Planchette had shot very wide of the mark in the supposed response to Mr. B.'s mental query, and hence was not prepared to be told that it was satisfactory, in proof of which Mr. B. wrote beneath it:

'Appropriate answer to my mental question, *Will my deceased wife communicate with me?*—I. A. B.'"

"May 28th. At the breakfast-table Mr. G. expressed a great desire to see Planchette perform, and she was brought from her box. Miss W. was also present. After several communications, Miss W. asked a mental question, and Planchette immediately wrote:

'Miss W., that is hardly possible in the present state of the money market; but later, I dare say you will accomplish what you desire to undertake.'

Miss W. 'Planchette is entirely off the track. My question was, *Can you tell me anything about my nephew?*'

Mr. G. 'Well, it is certainly very queer. *I* asked a mental question to which this is to a certain extent an answer.'

Mr. G. was seated beside me, thoroughly intent upon Planchette. Miss W. was at a distance, and not in any way *en rapport* with me. If this phenomenon of answering mental questions be clairvoyance, the situation of these two persons may account for the mixed nature of the answer, beginning with Miss W. and finishing with Mr. G."

Putnam's Monthly Magazine for December, 1868, contains an interesting article entitled "*Planchette in a New Character.*" What the "new character" is in which it appears, may be learned from the introductory paragraph, as follows:

"We, too, have a Planchette, and a Planchette with this signal merit: it disclaims all pretensions to supermundane inspirations; it operates freely—indeed, with extraordinary freedom; it goes at the tap of the drum. The first touch of the operators, no matter under what circumstances it is brought out to reveal its knowledge, sets it in motion. But it brings no communications from any celestial or spiritual sources. Its chirography is generally good, and frequently excellent. Its remarks evince an intelligence often above that of the operators, and its talent at answering or evading difficult questions is admirable. We have no theories about it."

It seems, from other passages in the article, that this Planchette disclaims the ability to tell anything that is not contained in the minds of the persons present, although it frequently gives theories in direct contradiction to the opinions of all present, and argues them with great persistence until driven up into a corner. It simply assumes the name of "Planchet," leaving off the feminine termination of the word; and "on being remonstrated with for illiteracy, it defended itself by saying, 'I always was a bad *speler*,'—an orthographical blunder," says the writer, "that no one in the room was capable of making."

Although the writer in the paragraph above quoted disclaims all theories on the subject, he does propound a theory, such as it is; but of this we defer our notice until we come to put the several theories that have been offered into the hopper and grind them up together; at which time we will take some further notice of the amusing peculiarities of this writer's Planchette.

The *Ladies' Repository* of November, 1868, contains an article, written by Rev. A. D. Field, entitled "Planchette; or, Spirit-Rapping Made Easy." This writer mentions a number of test questions asked by him of Planchette, the answers to which were all false. Yet he acknowledges that "the mysterious little creature called Planchette is no humbug; that some mysterious will-power causes it to answer questions, and that it is useless to ignore these things, or to laugh at them." The writer submits a theory by which he thinks these mysteries may be explained, in a measure, if not wholly, but this, with others, will be reserved for notice hereafter.

Harper's Monthly Magazine for December, 1868, contains an article entitled "*The Confessions of a Reformed Planchettist.*" In this article, the writer, no doubt drawing wholly or in part from his imagination, details a series of tricks which he had successfully practiced upon the credulity of others, and concludes by propounding a very sage and charitable theory to account for *all* Planchette phenomena, on which theory we shall yet have a word to offer.

Hours at Home, of February, 1869, contains an article, by J. T. Headley, entitled "*Planchette at the Confessional.*" In this article, the writer cogently argues the claims of these new phenomena upon the attention of scientific men. He says: "That it [the Planchette] writes things never dreamed of by the operators, is proved by their own testimony and the testimony of others, beyond all contradiction;" and goes so far as to assert that to whatever cause these phenomena may be attributed, "they will seriously affect the whole science of mental philosophy." He relates a number of facts, more or less striking, and propounds a theory in their explanation, to which, with others, we will recur by-and-by.

The foregoing are a few of the most noted, among the many less important, lucubrations that have fallen under our notice concerning this interesting subject—enough, however, to indicate the intense public interest which the performances of this little board are exciting. We will now proceed to notice some of the *theories* that have been advanced for the solution of the mystery.

THEORY FIRST—THAT THE BOARD IS MOVED BY THE HANDS THAT REST UPON IT.

It is supposed that this movement is made either by design or unconsciously, and that the answers are either the result of adroit guessing, or the expressions of some appropriate thoughts or memories which had been previously slumbering in the minds of the operators, and happen to be awakened at the moment.

After detailing his exploits (whether real or imaginary he has left us in doubt) in a successful and sustained course of deception, the writer in *Harper's* reaches this startling conclusion of the whole matter:

"It would only write when I moved it, and then it wrote precisely what I dictated. That persons write 'unconsciously,' I do not believe. As well tell me a man might pick pockets without knowing it. Nor am I at all prepared to believe the assertions of those who declare that they do not move the board. I know what operators will do in such cases; I know the distortion, the disregard of truth which association with this immoral board superinduces."

This writer has somewhat the advantage of me. I confess I have no means of coming to the knowledge of the truth but those of careful thought, patient observation, and collection of facts, and deduction from them. But here is a mind that can with one bold dive reach the inner mysteries of the sensible and supersensible world, penetrate the motives and impulses that govern the specific moral acts of men, and disclose at once to us the horrible secret of a conspiracy which, without preconcert, has been entered into by thousands of men, women, and children in all parts of the land, to cheat the rest of the human race—a conspiracy, too, in which certain members of innumerable private families have banded together to play tricks upon their fathers, mothers, brothers, and sisters! I feel awed by the overshadowing presence of such a mind—in fact, I do not feel quite *at home* with him, and therefore most respectfully bow myself out of his presence without further ceremony.

As to the hypothesis that the person or persons whose hands are on the board move it *unconsciously*, this is met by the fact that the persons are perfectly awake and in their senses, and are just as conscious of what they are doing or not doing as at any other time. Or if it be morally possible to suppose that they all, invariably, and with one accord, *lie* when they assert that the board moves without their volition, how is it that the answers which they give to questions, some of them mentally, are in so large a proportion of cases, *appropriate* answers? How is it, for example, that Planchette, under the hands of my own daughter, has, in numerous cases, given correctly the names of persons whom she had never seen or heard of before, giving also the names of their absent relatives, the places of their residence, etc., all of which were absolutely unknown by every person present except the questioner?

A theory propounded by the Rev. Dr. Patton, of Chicago, in an article published in *The Advance*, some time since, may be noticed under this head. He says:

"How, then, shall we account for the writing which is performed without any direct volition? Our method refers it to an automatic power of mind separate from conscious volition. * * * Very common is the experience of an automatic power in the pen, by which it finishes a word, or two or three words, after the thoughts have consciously gone on to what is to follow. We infer, then, from ordinary facts known to the habitual penman, that *if a fixed idea is in the mind* at the time when the nervous and volitional powers are exercised with a pen, it will often express itself spontaneously through the pen, when the mental faculties are at work otherwise. We suppose, then, that Planchette is simply an arrangement by which, through the outstretched arms and fingers, the mind comes into such relation with the delicate movements of the pencil, that its automatic power finds play, and the *ideas present in the mind are transferred unconsciously to paper.*" (Italics our own.)

That may all be, Doctor, and no marvel about it. That the "fixed idea"—"the ideas *present in the mind*," should be "transferred unconsciously to paper," by means of Planchette, is no more wonderful than that the same thing should be done by the pen, and *without* the intervention of that little board. But for the benefit of a sorely mystified world, be good enough to tell us how ideas that are *not* present, and that *never were* present, in the mind, can be transferred to paper by this automatic power of the mind. Grant that the mind possesses an automatic power to work in *grooves*, as it were, or in a manner in which it has been previously *trained* to work, as is illustrated by the delicate fingerings of the piano, all correct and skillful to the nicest shade, while the mind of the performer may for the moment be occupied in conversation; but not since the world began has there been an instance in which the mind, acting solely from itself, by "automatic powers" or otherwise, has been able to body forth any idea which was not previously within itself. That Planchette does sometimes write things of which the person or persons under whose hands it moves never had the slightest knowledge or even conception, it would be useless to deny.

THEORY SECOND—IT IS ELECTRICITY, OR MAGNETISM.

That electricity, or magnetism (a form of the same thing), is the agent of the production of these phenomena, is a theory which, perhaps, has more advocates among the masses than any other. It is the theory urged by Mr. Headley with a great amount of confidence in his article already referred to; and with his arguments, as those of an able and, in some sense, *representative* writer on this subject, we shall be principally occupied for a few paragraphs.

When this theory is offered in seriousness as a final solution of the mystery in question, we are tempted to ask, Who is electricity? what is his mental and moral *status?* and how and where did he get his education? Or if by "electricity" is here simply meant the subtile, imponderable, and *impersonal* fluid commonly known by that name, then let us ask, Who is at the other end of the wire?—for there must evidently be a *who* as well as a *what* in the case. But when the advocates of the electrical theory are brought to their strict definitions, they are compelled to admit that this agent is nothing more than a medium of the power and intelligence that are manifested. Now a medium, which signifies simply a *middle*, distinctly implies two opposite ends or extremes, and as applied in this case, one of those ends or extremes must be the source, and the other the recipient of the power or influence that is transmitted through the medium or middle; and it is an axiom of common sense that no medium can be a perfect medium which has anything to do with the origination or qualification of that which is intended simply to flow through it, or which is not absolutely free from action except as it is acted upon. That there are so-called mediums which refract, pervert, falsify, or totally obliterate the characteristics of that which was intended to be transmitted through them, is not to be denied; but these are by no means perfect or reliable mediums, either in physical or psychic matters.

If the little instrument in question, therefore, is, through the medium of electricity or any other agency, brought under perfect control and then driven to write a communication, the force that drives and the intelligence that directs it can not be attributed to the medium itself, but to something behind and beyond it which must embrace *in itself* all the active powers and qualifications to produce the effect. Now let us see where Mr. Headley gets the active powers and qualifications to produce the phenomena manifested by his Planchette. He shall speak for himself:

"That a spirit, good or bad, has anything to do with this piece of board and the tips of children's fingers, is too absurd a supposition to be entertained for a moment. We are driven, therefore, to the conclusion that what is written (by honest operators) has its origin either in the minds of those whose hands are on the instrument, or else it results from communication with other minds through another channel than the outward senses. At all events, on this hypothesis I have been able to explain most of the phenomena I have witnessed. I had, with others, laughed at the stories told about Planchette, when a lady visiting my family from the city brought, as the latest novelty, one for my daughter. Experiments were of course made with it, with very little success, till a young lady came to visit us from the West, whose efforts with those of my son wrought a marvelous change. She was modest and retiring, with a rich brown complexion, large swimming eyes, dark as midnight, and a dreamy expression of countenance, and altogether a temperament that is usually found to possess great magnetic power. My son, on the contrary, is fair, full of animal life, and enjoying everything with the keenest relish. In short, they were as opposite in all respects as two beings could well be. As the phenomena produced by electricity are well known to arise from opposite poles, or differently charged bodies, they would naturally be adapted to the trial of Planchette."

Mr. H. now finds the mysterious agency, "electricity," completely unchained, and under the hands of this couple Planchette becomes "very active." Indifferent to its performances at first, he was induced to give it more serious attention by the correct answers given to a couple of questions asked in a joking manner by his wife, concerning some love affairs of his before they were married, and which were known to none present except himself and wife. Of course these answers, being in his wife's mind when she asked the question, were supposed to be "communicated through the agency of electricity or magnetism to the two operators," and the mystery was thus summarily disposed of. But an interest being thus for the first time aroused in Mr. H.'s mind, he proceeds to inquire a little further into the peculiarities of this new phenomenon, and proceeds as follows:

"Seeing that Planchette was so familiarly acquainted with my lady friends, I asked it point blank: 'Where is Mary C——?' This was a friend of my early youth and later manhood, who had always seemed to me rather a relative than an acquaintance. To my surprise it answered, 'Nobody knows.'

I supposed I knew, because for twenty years she had lived on the Hudson River in summer, and in New York in the winter.

'Is she happy?' I asked. 'Better be dead,' was the reply.
'Why?' 'Unhappy' was written out at once.
'What makes her unhappy?' 'Won't tell.'
'Is she in fault, or others?' 'Partly herself.'

I now pushed questions in all shapes, but they were evaded. At last I asked, 'How many brothers has she?'

'One,' was the response. 'That,' said I, 'is false;' but not having heard from the family for several years, I asked again, 'How many *did* she have?' '*Three.*' 'Where are the other two?' I continued. 'Dead.'

'What is the name of the living one?' 'John.' I could not recollect that either of them bore this name, but afterward remembered it was that of the eldest. Now I had no means of ascertaining whether this was all true, but convinced it was not, I began to ask ridiculous and vexatious questions, when the answers showed excessive irritation, and finally it wrote '*Devil.*' I then said: 'Who are you?' 'Brother of the Devil.'

'What is your occupation?' 'Tending fires.'
'What are you going to do with me?' 'Broil you.'
'What for?' 'Wicked.'

Now while I was excessively amused at all this, I noticed that the two young operators were greatly agitated, and begged me to stop. I saw at a glance that the very superstitious feeling that I was endeavoring to ridicule away, was creeping over them, and I desisted. . . . Another day I asked where a certain gentleman was who failed years ago, taking in his fall a considerable amount of my own funds. I said 'Where is Mr. Green?' 'In Brazil.'

'Will he ever pay me anything?' 'Yes.'
'When?' 'Next year.'
'How much.' 'Ten thousand dollars.'

Neither of the operators knew anything about this affair, and the answer, 'Brazil,' was so out of the way and unexpected, that all were surprised. Whether the man was there or not, I could not tell, nor did I know if he ever had been there—indeed, the last time I heard from him he was in New York."

Now, observing that no conscious or intelligent agency in shaping these answers is assigned to the young persons whose hands were upon the board, and who, it appears, did not know anything of the persons concerning whom the inquiries were made, it would, perhaps, as we desire nothing but a true philosophy on this matter, be worth while to look a little critically at the answers and statements that were given, and the further explanations propounded by Mr. H. For convenience, they may be classified as follows:

1. Answers that were substantially in the interrogator's own mind when he asked the questions. Such were the answers to the questions: "How many brothers *did* she [Mary C——] have?" "Where did she *formerly* live?" He tells us that "the pencil slowly wrote out in reply: '*Catkill*,' leaving out the *s;*" and adds: "of course, this place was in my mind, though neither of the young people knew anything about the lady or her residence."

2. Answers which he does not know were in his mind, but supposes they must have been. Thus, in his own language, while commenting on the answers to questions respecting Mary C—— and her brothers: "Nor can I account for the answer ' *Unhappy*,' *unless unconsciously to myself* there passed through my mind that vague fear so common to us all when we inquire about friends of whom we have not heard for years. The death of the two brothers baffled all conjecture *unless I remembered* that during the war I saw the death of a young man of the same name, and I wondered at the time if it was one of these brothers—whether they had joined the army." (The Italics our own.) So also of Planchette's answers to the questions respecting Mr. Green, locating him in Brazil, and saying that he intended to pay him (Mr. H.) ten thousand dollars next year, while Mr. G. had last been reported to Mr. H. as being in New York, and the latter did not know that he had ever been in Brazil. But Mr. H., after thinking over a certain conversation which he had previously had with Mr. Green respecting a business journey he had made to "*South America*," remarks: "Brazil doubtless often occurred to me—in fact, I was conscious on reflection that I had more frequently located him in that country than in any other. So when the question was put, it would involuntarily flash over me *without my being conscious of it,* 'I wonder if he has gone back to South America, and if his venture is in Brazil?' *Magnetism caught up the flashing thought and put it on paper.*" (Italics our own.) Such is his hypothesis to explain an hypothesis!

3. Answers which he not only knows he had not in his mind when the questions were asked, but which were directly *contrary* to his mind or opinion. Such were answers to several of the questions occurring in the conversation about Mary C——, as, "better be dead;" "unhappy;" fault "partly herself;" has "*one*" brother; which latter statement was so directly contrary to his mind that he even pronounced it "false," **until he** thought to inquire, "How many *did* she have?"

4. Answers which were not only not in his mind, but which he directly pronounces "*false*," and thus dismisses them. Such, for instance, is the answer "Nobody knows," to the question "Where is Mary C——?" "That this," says he, "was false, is evident on the very face of it."

With this analysis of the leading phenomena cited by Mr. H. before us, let us look at the wonderful things which "electricity and magnetism" are made to accomplish.

I do not dispute that there is such a power of the human mind as that known as clairvoyance. I have had too many proofs of this to doubt it. But I have had equally positive proofs that the development of its phenomena is dependent upon certain necessary conditions, among which are, that the agent of them, in order to be able to reveal the secret thoughts of another, must possess by nature peculiar nervous susceptibilities, enabling his psychic emanations, so to speak, to sympathetically coalesce with those of the person whose thoughts and internal mental states are to be the subject of investigation. But this sympathetic coalescence can not take place where there is the slightest psychic repulsion or antagonism to the clairvoyant on the part of the interrogating party. Moreover, even when all these conditions are present, nothing can be correctly read from the mind of the questioner unless there is on his mind a *clear and distinct definition* of the matters of which he seeks to be told.

But even in class No. 1 of the above series we find that "electricity," hitherto believed to be only an imponderable and impersonal fluid, has, upon Mr. H.'s theory, been able to accomplish the revealment of secret thoughts entirely independent of all these conditions. It is distinctly stated that those young persons whose hands were on the Planchette knew nothing whatever of the matters which formed the several subjects of inquiry; and for aught that is stated to the contrary, they appear to have been perfectly awake and in their normal state. In addition to this, it is to be observed that Mr. Headley here appears in the assumed character of a captious, contentious, and somewhat irritating questioner, which, whether he intended it or not, was entirely the opposite of that harmonious and sympathetic interflow of mental states known in other cases to be necessary to a successful clairvoyant diagnosis of inward thoughts. And yet "electricity" overleaps all these obstacles, seizes facts that occurred many years previous, some of which were known only to Mr. H. and wife, others only to Mr. H. himself, and instantly flashes forth the appropriate answer! Here is science! If there were no other phenomena connected with Planchette, this alone might well challenge the attention of philosophers!

But if this is wonderful, what shall we think of the achievements of this same "electricity" and "magnetism" in revealing facts of the second class—facts which the questioner himself did not and does not now *know* were in his mind, but only *supposes they must have been?* Think of a diffused element of nature, which from the dawn of creation had been blind and dead, and only passively obedient to certain laws of equilibrium, suddenly assuming intelligence and volition, burrowing into a man's brains, rummaging among ten thousand thoughts, emotions, and experiences stored up in the archives of his memory, and finally coming to the mere fossil of a (*supposed*) experience from which the last vestige of memory-life had departed, and seizing this incident, it moves the little board with an intelligent volition, and lo, the fact stands revealed.

And again, what of that spicy colloquy in which Planchette writes the words "devil," "devil's brother," "stir fires," "broil you," etc.? Oh, Mr. H. tells us, "That was owing to the irritation of the mediums, their horror and fright, their superstition, and their repugnance to the questions that were being asked." Curious, is it not? to see "electricity" seizing hold of this irritation, that horror, the other fright, and such and such a superstition, repugnance, and disgust, and, carefully arranging these mental emotions, building them up by a mysterious mason-work into a distinctly defined and sharply pronounced individuality, with a peculiar moral and intellectual character of its own, differing more from each and all of the parties present in the flesh than any one of the latter differed from another! And this individuality, too, putting forth a volition which was not *their* volition, moving the Planchette which *they* did not move, making and arranging letters which *they* did not make and arrange, writing intelligent words and sentences which *they* did not write, and then causing this creation to assume the name and character of a regularly built "devil"—a character which appears to have been so far from these young persons' minds that they were unwilling to look it in the face, and were sorely afraid of it! Surely, if "electricity" can do all this, then "electricity" itself is the "devil," and the less mankind have to do with it the better.

But more wonderful still. It appears that "electricity" can give answers, of which not even the slightest elements previously existed in the mind of the questioner or any of the company, and which were even diametrically *contrary* to his mind; as in the answers of class No. 3. Here "electricity" swings loose, and, becoming completely independent, commences business on its "own hook." Not only so, but it even goes so far beyond the sphere of Mr. H.'s mind as to *fib* a little, giving at least two answers which this writer pronounced "false," as noted in class No 4—thus giving a still more signal display of its independent powers of invention—naughty invention though it was.

Seriously, had not friend Headley better employ his fine talents in giving us another clever book or two about "Washington and his Generals," and leave Mr. Planchette, and that more wonderful personage, Mr. Electricity, to take care of themselves? We are obliged here to part company with Mr. H., and pass on for the purpose of having a few words under this same head with the reverend author of "Planchette, or Spirit-Rapping Made Easy," in the *Ladies' Repository*.

I find it difficult to get at the idea of this writer, if indeed he himself has any definite idea on the subject. By the title of his article, however, and several expressions that occur in the body of it, he seems to associate the performances of the Planchette with a somewhat extensive class of phenomena, in which spirit-rappings, table-tippings, etc., are included. He says:

"Twelve years ago I took pains to study the matter, and at that time I came to conclusions that are every day being proved to be true. I was soon satisfied that as regarded 'trance mediums,' the cause was due to one-third trickery, one-third partial insanity or monomania, and the remainder animal magnetism. I have since learned that opium and hashish (Indian hemp) played an important part. It was proved that young ladies purchased written speeches which they delivered under the influence of hashish."

He then goes on to speak of galvanism, magnetism, electricity, animal magnetism, and the odylic force; but, so far as we can see, without proving any necessary connection between these forces or either of them, and the subject which he aims to elucidate. Quoting a former article of his, he continues:

"The magnetizer of whom I spoke [an exposer of rappings] threw himself into magnetic connection with the table, and *willed* it to move hither and thither. The will in this case seemed to be a powerful battery, putting its subject into life. Now I suggest that this power be applied to machinery. We will get us a large propelling wheel, to which we will connect our machinery. We will then engage a company of mediums who shall get into *rapport* with one wheel, and stand willing the wheel on in its evolutions. . . . If a table may be made to spin around the room, why may not a wheel be made to turn as well?"

The writer certainly deserves credit for this sage suggestion, and a patent for his machine; but whether he will succeed in making it operate satisfactorily without calling into requisition the "monomania," the "hashish," and the "opium," remains to be seen. He then goes on to describe Planchette, and afterward continues:

"The mysterious little creature is called Planchette, and is no humbug. And it conforms to all the customs of the old-time tipping-tables. The operator magnetizes Planchette, and by a mysterious will-power causes it to answer questions. Before giving illustrations, we may as well state the laws that seem to govern it. *First.* It will always answer correctly, *if the operator knows the answer. Second.* While it will answer other questions, in all the experiments I have ever engaged in, it has never answered correctly. *Third.* If a person standing by, who has strong magnetic powers, asks a question, Planchette will answer. But *in all cases*, in our experiments, some ruling mind must have knowledge of what the answer should be, if a correct answer is returned."

In reply to the above, we assert, *First.* That the "operator" does not "magnetize" the board at all, nor does he exercise any "will power" over it, causing it to answer questions; and if he did thus cause it to answer only those questions whose answers are already in his mind, what marvel is there in it, more than there is in my pen being caused by my will-power to trace these words and sentences? *Secondly*. If by his *second* and *third* specifications of the supposed "laws" which govern Planchette, he means to imply that it will not tell, *often* tell, and tell with remarkable correctness, things that were never known or dreamed of by the operator, the questioner, or any one present in visible form, then he simply mistakes, as can be testified by thousands, in the most positive manner. But the great essential question is, not so much whether answers given under such and such circumstances can be *correct*, as whether answers and communications *can be given at all*, which have no origin in the minds of the persons engaged in the experiment, and which must hence be referred to some outside intelligence?

The writer under review, after all, acknowledges his incompetency to unravel this subject, by saying:

"There are mysteries in Planchette. No one is ready to explain the mysterious connection between the mind and the little machine, but there can no longer be any doubt that these curious phenomena, table-tipping and all, are produced by magnetism and electricity. . . . It is useless to ignore these things, or to laugh at them. It were better to account for them, and subject the influence to the power of man. . . . When some scientific man will condescend to toy with Planchette, we shall have the curtain drawn aside behind which the spirits have operated these years, and this calamitous spirit-rapping mania will destroy no longer."

One might almost regret that this latter thought did not occur to the writer before he commenced his article, in which case, by a little patient waiting for this ideal and very condescending "scientific man," we might have been spared this diatribe of jumbled electricity, magnetism, will-power, opium, hashish, monomania, and driving wheels.

ELECTRICITY HAS NOTHING TO DO WITH IT.

From much and varied observation and experiment in reference to the performances of Planchette, and of kindred phenomena, now extending over a period of about twenty years, I here record my denial, in the most emphatic manner, that electricity or magnetism, properly so called, has anything to do with the mystery at all, and call for the proof that it has. That a certain psycho-dynamic agency closely allied to, and in some of its modifications perhaps identical with, Reichenbach's "Od," or odylic force, may have some mediatorial part to play in the affair, I do not dispute, nor yet, for the present, do I affirm. But though this agency has sometimes been identified with what, for the want of a better term, has been called "animal magnetism," it has yet to be proved, I believe, that there are any of the properties of the magnet, or of magnetism, about it, even so much as would suffice to attract the most comminuted iron filings. It is remarkable that the assertion or hypothesis that electricity or magnetism is concerned in the production of the phenomena in question, has never yet had an origin in any high scientific authority. This is accounted for by the fact that those who are properly acquainted with this agency, and who have the proper apparatus at their command, can demonstrate the truth or falsity of such a hypothesis with the greatest ease. For an experiment, place your Planchette upon a plate of glass, or some other non-conducting substance. Attach to it a common pith-ball electrometer, and then let your medium place his hands upon the board. If electricity equal to the force even of a small fraction of a grain passes from the medium to the board, the pith ball, to that extent, will be deflected from its position. By means of the *Torsion Balance* electrometer, invented by Coulomb, the presence of almost the smallest conceivable fraction of a grain of electrical force in your Planchette or your table might be detected; and with these delicate tests within reach, tell us not that the movements in question are caused by electricity till you have *proved* it positively and beyond all dispute.

In the discussion of this electrical theory we have occupied more space than we originally intended, but we have thought it might be for the interest of true science to exhibit, once for all, this ridiculous and yet very popular fallacy, in its true light.

THIRD—THE DEVIL THEORY.

This theory, which appears to have many advocates, is well set forth in the following excerpts from an article published in the Philadelphia *Universe*, a Catholic organ:

"Neither the sight of the eye, nor the touch of the hand, can discover the spring by which Planchette moves. Therefore it is not, in its movements, a toy. It moves—undoubtedly it moves. And how? Intelligently! It answers questions of any kind put to it in any language required. It does this. This can not be done but by intelligence. Well, by what description of intelligence? It can not be supposed that the Divine intelligence is the motive; for how can God be conceived to make such a manifestation of himself as Planchette exhibits?

"A corresponding reason cuts off the idea that it is presided over by an angelic intelligence; and it is evident to all that a human mind does not control it. There is but one more character of intelligence—that of evil spirits. Therefore Planchette is moved by the agents of hell. . . . But why should the devil connect himself with Planchette? . . . We suppose that the experienced scoundrel is ready to do anything human wickedness may ask him when souls are the price of the condescension. But his reasons for particular manifestations are of small importance here. Facts are facts, and the point is, that Planchette is not a toy, that it is moved by an intelligence, and that the intelligence that moves it is necessarily evil. We would therefore advise all who have a Planchette to build for it a special fire of pitch and brimstone. . . . No one has a right to consult the enemy of God. They who do so are in danger of becoming worshipers of the devil, and of dwelling with him for ever."

This theory has at least the merit of being clear, definite, and easy to be understood, if it is not in all respects convincing. But here we have an exemplification of the old paradox of an irresistible force coming in contact with an immovable body. The Catholic priest tells us that

Planchette is *not* a toy; that it moves by an intelligence and volition that is not human; that its moving and directing power is of the devil. The Rev. Dr. Patton, in his article in the *Advance* (heretofore referred to), tells us that "It is a philanthropic toy, which may be used to bring to light hidden connections of mind and body, and to refute the assumptions of spiritism;" and the Rev. A. D. Field, in his article in the *Ladies' Repository*, backs up Dr. Patton by saying, that it is "a mere toy," "is no humbug," is of "some use;"—and, concerning the *devil* theory of the general power which moves it and other physical bodies, he says: there is "too often the spirit of gentleness to make the theory acceptable." The "immovable body" here, is the authority of the Catholic priest; the "irresistible force" is the authority of our clerical brethren representing Protestantism; and after this fair impingement of the latter upon the former, we shall, perhaps, have to adopt a compromise solution of the problem, by saying that the "immovable body" has been moved *a little*, and that the "irresistible force" has been resisted *some*.

But this *devil* theory, if what the Bible teaches us concerning that personage is true, is encumbered with other difficulties; and the first of these is, that the devil, however wicked, is not a *fool*. If he should set a trap for human souls, he would not be so stupid as to tell them there is a trap there. When approaching human beings, he assumes, as the good book tells us, the garb of an angel of light; but it is not likely that he would ever say he is the devil, as Planchette sometimes does—at least until he felt quite sure of his prey. And again, when, in a case slightly parallel with cases sometimes involved in the question in hand, the captious Pharisees accused the Saviour of men of casting out devils by Beelzebub the prince of devils, he reminded them that a house or a kingdom divided against itself can not stand. Now Planchette, I admit, is not always a saint—in fact, she sometimes talks and acts very naughtily as well as foolishly; yet at other times, when a better *spirit* takes possession of her, she is gentle, loving, well disposed, and does certainly give most excellent advice,—advice which could not be heeded without detriment to the devil's kingdom, and which, if universally followed, would work its overthrow entirely. It is inconceivable that Satan would thus tear down with one hand what he builds up with another. But just at this point I wish to say, I think there is need of great caution in consulting Planchette on matters of a weighty or serious nature, lest one should extort from her mere *confirmations* of his own errors, either in doctrine or practice; and that nothing should in any case be accepted from it that is repugnant to the established principles of the Christian religion. But we are after the *science* of the thing now, and for the present that is our only question—a question, however, which the devil theory, as will appear from the foregoing, does not seem fully to answer.

THEORY OF A FLOATING, AMBIENT MENTALITY.

It is supposed by those who hold this theory, or rather hypothesis, that the assumed floating, ambient mentality is an aggregate emanation from the minds of those present in the circle; that this mentality is clothed, by some mysterious process, with a force analogous to what it possesses in the living organism, by which force it is enabled, under certain conditions, to move physical bodies and write or otherwise express its thoughts; and that in its expression of the combined intelligence of the circle, it generally follows the strongest mind, or the mind that is otherwise best qualified or conditioned to give current to the thought. Although the writer of the interesting article, entitled "*Planchette in a New Character*," in *Putnam's Monthly* for December, 1868, disclaims, at the commencement of his lucubration, all theories on the subject, yet, after collating his facts, he shows a decided leaning to the foregoing theory as the nearest approach to a satisfactory explanation. "Floating, combined intelligence brought to bear upon an inanimate object," "active intellectual principle afloat in the circumambient air," are the expressions he uses as probably affording some light on the subject. This is a thought on which, as concerns its main features, many others have rested, not only in this country but in Europe, especially in England, as I am told by a friend who recently visited several sections of Great Britain where forms of these mysterious phenomena prevail.

The first difficulty that stands in the way of this hypothesis is that it supposes a thing which, if true, is quite as mysterious and inexplicable as the mystery which it purports to explain. How is it that an "intellectual principle" can detach itself from an intellectual being, of whose personality it formed the chief ingredient, and become an outside, objective, "floating," and "circumambient" entity, with a capability of thinking, willing, acting, and expressing thought, in which the original possessor of the emanated principle often has no conscious participation? And after you have told us this, then tell us how the "intellectual principle," not only of *one*, but of *several* persons can emanate from them, become "floating" and "ambient," and then, losing separate identity, *conjoin* and form *one* active communicating agent with the powers aforesaid? And after you have removed from these *mere assumptions* the aspect of physical and moral impossibility, you will have another task to perform, and that is to show us how this emanated, "combined," "floating," "circumambient" intelligence can sometimes assume an individual and seemingly *personal* character of its own, totally distinct from, and, in some features, even *antagonistic* to, all the characters in the circle in which the "emanation" is supposed to have its origin?

It is not denied now that the answers and communications of Planchette (and of the influence acting through other channels) often do exhibit a controlling influence of the mind of the medium or of other persons in the circle. But no theory should ever be considered as explaining a mystery unless it covers the *whole ground* of that mystery. Even, therefore, should we consider the theory of the "floating intelligence" of the circle reproducing itself in expression, as explaining that part of the phenomenon which identifies itself with the minds of the circle (which it does not), what shall be said of those cases in which the phenomena exhibit characteristics which are *sui generis*, and can not possibly have been derived from the minds of the circle?

That phenomena of the latter class are sometimes exhibited is not only proved by many other facts that might be cited, but is clearly exemplified by this same writer in *Putnam's Magazine*. The intelligence whose performances and communications he relates seems to stand out with a character and individuality as strongly marked and as distinct from any and all in the circle as any one of them was distinct from another. This individuality was first shown by giving its own pet names to the different persons composing the circle—"Flirt," "Clarkey," "Hon. Clarke," "The Angel," and "Sassiness." The young lady designated by the last *sobriquet*, after it had been several times repeated, petitioned to be indicated thereafter "only by the initial 'S,'" which the impertinent scribbler accorded only so far as omitting all the letters except the five S's, so that she was afterward recognized as "S.S.S.S.S."

The writer further says:

"It is always respectful to 'Hon. Clarke,' and when pressed to state what it thought of him, answered that he was 'a good skipper,' a reputation fairly earned by his capacity for managing a fleet of small boats. But we were not contented with so vague an answer, and our urgent demand for an analysis of his character produced the reply: 'A native crab apple, but spicy and sweet when ripe.' * * * When asked to go on, it wrote: 'Ask me Hon. Clarke's character again, and I will flee to the realms of imperishable woe; or, as Tabitha is here, say I'll pull your nose;' and on being taunted with its incapacity to fulfill the threat, it wrote: 'Metaphorically speaking, of course.' Not satisfied with this rebuff, on another occasion the subject was again pursued, and the answer elicited as follows: 'Yes, but you can't fool me. I said nay once, and when I says nay I means nay.' [A mind of *its own*, then.] More than once it has lapsed into the same misuse of the verb, as: 'I not only believes it, but I knows it;' and again: 'You asks and I answers, because I am here.' * * *

"Again, on being remonstrated with for illiteracy, it defended itself by saying: 'I always was a bad speler' (*sic*); an orthographical blunder that no one in the room was capable of making. But on the whole, our Planchette is a scientific and cultivated intelligence, of more than average order, though it may be, at times, slightly inaccurate in orthography, and occasionally quote incorrectly; I must even confess that there are moments when its usual elegance of diction lapses into slang terms and abrupt contradictions. But, after all, though we flatter ourselves that as a family we contain rather more than ordinary intelligence, still it is more than a match for us."

Who can fail to perceive, from these quotations and admissions, the marked and distinctive *individuality* of the intelligence that was here manifested, as being of itself totally fatal to the idea of derivation from the circle?

But not only was this intelligence *distinctive*, but in several instances even *antagonistic* to that existing in the circle, as in the case reported as follows:

"Some one desiring to pose this ready writer, asked for its theory of the Gulf Stream; which it announced without hesitation to be 'Turmoil in the water produced by conglomeration of icebergs.' Objection was made that the warmth of the waters of the natural phenomenon rather contradicted this original view of the subject; to which Planchette tritely responded: 'Friction produces heat.' 'But how does friction produce heat in this case?' pursued the questioner. 'Light a match,' was the inconsequent answer—Planchette evidently believing that the pupil was ignorant of first principles. 'But the Gulf Stream flows north; how, then, can the icebergs accumulate at its source?' was the next interrogation; which elicited the contemptuous reply: 'There is as much ice and snow at the south pole as at the north, ignorant Clarkey.' 'But it flows from the Gulf of Mexico?' pursued the undismayed. 'You've got me there, unless it flows underground,' was the cool and unexpected retort; and it wound up by declaring, sensibly, that, after all, 'it is a meeting of the north and south Atlantic currents, which collide, and the eddie (*sic*) runs northward.' [At another time,] on being twice interrogated in regard to a subject, it replied tartly: 'I hate to be asked if I am sure of a fact.'"

Now, what could have been this intelligence which thus insisted upon preserving and asserting its individuality so distinctly as to forbid all reasonable hypothesis of a compounded derivation from the minds of the circle, even were such a thing possible? A fairy, perhaps, snugly cuddled up under the board so as to elude observation. Friend "Clarkey," try again, for surely *this* time you are a little befogged, or else the present writer is *more* so.

"TO DAIMONION" (THE DEMON).

There was published, several years ago, by Gould & Lincoln, Boston, a little work entitled: "TO DAIMONION, OR THE SPIRITUAL MEDIUM. *Its nature illustrated by the history of its uniform mysterious manifestations when unduly excited.* By TRAVERSE OLDFIELD." This author deals largely in quotations from ancient writers in illustration of his subject; and as an attempt to explain the mysteries of clairvoyance, trance, second-sight, "spirit-knockings," intelligent movements of physical bodies without hands, etc., his work has claims to our attention which do not usually pertain to the class of works to which it belongs. "*To Daimonion*" (the demon), or the "spiritual medium," he supposes to be the *spiritus mundi*, or the spirit of the universe, which formed so large an element in the cosmological theories of many ancient philosophers; and this, "when unduly excited" (whatever that may mean), he supposes to be the medium, not only of many psychic and apparently preternatural phenomena described in the writings of all previous ages, but also of the similar phenomena of modern times, of which it is now admitted that Planchettism is only one of the more recently developed phases. For some reason, which seemed satisfactory to him, but which we fear he has not made clear or convincing to the mass of his readers, this writer assumes it as more than probable that this *spiritus mundi*—a living essence which surrounds and pervades the world, and even the whole universe—is identical with the "nervous principle" which connects the soul with the body,—in all this unconsciously reaffirming nearly the exact theory first propounded by Mesmer, in explanation of the phenomena of "animal magnetism," so called. Quotations are given from Herodotus, Xenophon, Cicero, Pliny, Galen, and many others, referring to phenomena well known in the times in which these several writers lived, and which he supposes can be explained only on the general hypothesis here set forth; and in the same category of marvels, to be explained in the same way, he places the performances of the snake-charmers, clairvoyants, thought-readers, etc., of modern Egypt and India.

This *spiritus mundi*, or "nervous principle," to which he supposes the ancients referred when they spoke of "the demon," is, according to his theory, the medium, or menstruum, by which, under certain conditions of "excitement," the thoughts and potencies of one mind, with its affections, emotions, volitions, etc., flow into another, giving rise to reflex expressions, which, to persons ignorant of this principle, have seemed possible only as the utterances of outside and supermundane intelligences. And as this same *spiritus mundi*, or demon, pervades and connects the mind equally with all *physical* bodies, in certain *other* states of "excitement" it moves those physical bodies, or makes sounds upon them, expressing intelligence—that intelligence always being a reflex of the mind of the person who, consciously or unconsciously, served as the exciting agent.

Whatever elements of truth this theory, in a *different* mode of application, might be found to possess, in the form in which it is here presented it is encumbered by two or three difficulties which altogether seem fatal. In the first place, it wears upon its face the appearance of a thing "fixed up" to meet an emergency, and which would never have been thought of except by a mind pressed almost to a state of desperation by the want of a theory to account for a class of facts. Look at it: "The spirit of the world identical with the nervous principle"!—the same, "when unduly *excited*," the medium by which a mind may *unconsciously* move other minds and organisms, or even dead matter, in the expression of its own thoughts! Where is the shadow of proof? Is it anything more than the sheerest assumption?

Then again: even if this mere assumption were admitted for truth, it would not account for that large class of facts referred to in the course of our remarks on the "Electrical theory," unless this *spiritus mundi*, demon, nervous principle, or spiritual medium, is made at once not only the "medium," but the intelligent and designing *source* of the communication; for, as we have said before, it would be perfectly useless to deny that thoughts are sometimes communicated through the Planchette and similar channels, which positively never had any existence in the minds of any of the persons visibly present.

And then, too, in relation to the nature of the demon, or demons: the theory of the ancients, from whose representative minds this writer has quoted, was notoriously quite different from that which he has given. The ancients recognized good demons and evil demons. The demon of Socrates was regarded by him as an invisible, individual intelligence. A legion of demons were in one instance cast out by Christ from the body of a man whom they had infested; we can hardly suppose that these were simply a legion of "nervous principles" or "souls of the world." What those demons were really understood to be in those days, may be learned from a passage in the address of Titus to his army, when encamped before Jerusalem, in which, in order to remove from their minds the fear of death in battle, he says:

"For what man of virtue is there who does not know that those souls which are severed from their fleshy bodies in battles by the sword, are received by the ether, that purest of elements, and joined to that company which are placed among the stars; that they become *good demons* and propitious heroes, and show themselves as such to their posterity afterward?"—*Josephus, Wars of the Jews, B. VI., chap.* 1, *sec.* 5.

Hesiod and many others might be quoted to the same purpose; but let this suffice as to the character and origin of these demons; and it may suffice also for the theory of *To Daimonion*, as to the particular mystery here to be explained.

IT IS SOME PRINCIPLE OF NATURE AS YET UNKNOWN.

If there is any wisdom in this theory, it is so profound that we "don't see it." It looks very much to us as though this amounted only to the saying that "all we know about the mystery is, that it is *unknown;* all the explanation that we can give of it is, that it is inexplicable; and that the only theory of it is, that it has no theory." Thus it leaves the matter just where it was before, and we should not have deemed this saying worthy of the slightest notice had we not heard and read so much grave discussion on the subject, criticising almost every other theory, and then concluding with the complacent announcement of the writer's or speaker's theory as superior to all others, that "*it is some principle or force of nature as yet unknown!*"

THEORY OF THE AGENCY OF DEPARTED SPIRITS.

This theory apparently has both merits and difficulties, which at present we can only briefly notice. Among the strong points in its favor, the first and most conspicuous one is, that it accords with what this mysterious intelligence, in all its numerous forms of manifestation, has steadily, against all opposition, persisted in claiming *for itself*, from its first appearance, over twenty years ago, till this day. And singularly enough, it appears as a fact which, perhaps, should be stated as a portion of the history of these phenomena, that years before public attention and investigation were challenged by the first physical manifestation that claimed a spiritual origin, an approaching and general revisitation of departed human spirits was, in several instances, the burden of *remarkable predictions*. I have in my possession a little book, or bound pamphlet, entitled, "A Return of Departed Spirits," and bearing the imprint, "Philadelphia: Published by J. R. Colon, 203½ Chestnut Street, 1843," in which is contained an account of strange phenomena which occurred among the Shakers at New Lebanon, N. Y., during the early part of that year. In the language of the author: "Disembodied spirits began to take possession of the bodies of the brethren and sisters; and thus, by using them as instruments, made themselves known by speaking through the individuals whom they had got into." The writer then goes on to describe what purported to be the visitations of hundreds in that way, from different nations and tribes that had lived on earth in different ages —the consistency of the phenomena being maintained throughout. I have conversed with leading men among the Shakers of the United States concerning this affair, and they tell me that the visitation was not confined to New Lebanon, but extended, more or less, to all the Shaker communities in the United States—not spreading from one to another, but appearing nearly simultaneously in all. They also tell me that the phenomena ceased about as suddenly as they appeared; and that when the brethren were assembled, by previous appointment, to take leave of their spirit-guests, they were exhorted by the latter to treasure up these things in their hearts; to say nothing about them to the world's people, but to wait patiently, and soon they (the spirits) would return, and make their presence known to the world generally.

During the interval between the autumn of 1845 and the spring of 1847, a book, wonderful for its inculcations both of truth and error, was dictated in the mesmeric state by an uneducated boy—A. J. Davis—in which the following similar prediction occurs:

"It is a truth that spirits commune with one another while one is in the body and the other in the higher spheres—and this, too, when the person in the body is unconscious of the influx, and hence can not be convinced of the fact; and this truth will ere long present itself in the form of a living demonstration. And the world will hail with delight the ushering in of that era when the interiors of men will be opened, and the spiritual communion will be established, such as is now being enjoyed by the inhabitants of Mars, Jupiter, and Saturn."—*Nat. Div. Rev., pp.* 675, 676.

Eight months after the book containing this passage was published, and more than a year after the words here quoted were dictated and written, strange rapping sounds were heard in an obscure family in an obscure village in the western part of New York. On investigation, those sounds were found to be connected with intelligence, which, rapping at certain letters of the alphabet as it was called over, spelled sentences, and claimed to be a *spirit*. The phenomena increased, assumed many other forms, extended to other mediums, and rapidly spread, not only all over this country, but over the civilized world. And wherever this intelligence has been interrogated under conditions which *itself* prescribes for proper answers, its great leading and persistent response to the question, "What are you?" has been, "*We are spirits!*" Candor also compels us to admit that this claim has been perseveringly maintained against the combined opposition of the great mass of intelligent and scientific minds to whom the world has looked for its guidance; and so successfully has it been maintained, that its converts are now numbered by millions, gathered, not from the ranks of the ignorant and superstitious, but consisting mostly of the intelligent and thinking middle classes, and of many persons occupying the highest positions in civil and social life.

At first its opponents met it with expressions of utter contempt and cries of "humbug." Many ingenious and scientific persons volunteered their efforts to expose the "trick;" and if they seemed, in some instances, to meet with momentary success in solving the mystery, the next day would bring with it some *new* form of the phenomenon to which none of their theories would apply. Being finally discouraged by repeated failures to explain the hidden cause of these wonders, they withdrew from the field, and for many years allowed the matter to go by default; and only within the last twelvemonth has investigation of the subject been re-aroused by the introduction into this country of the little instrument called "the Planchette"—an instrument which, to our certain knowledge, was used at least ten years ago in France, and that, too, as a supposed means of communicating with departed spirits.

This little board has been welcomed as a "toy" or a "game" into thousands of families, without suspicion of its having the remotest connection with so-called "Spiritualism." The cry has been raised,

"Quidquid id est, timeo Danaos et dona ferentes,"

but too late! The Trojan walls are everywhere down; the wooden horse is already dragged into the city with all the armed heroes concealed in its bowels; the battle has commenced, and must be fought out to the bitter end, as best it may be; and in the numerous magazine and newspaper articles that have lately appeared on the subject, we have probably only the beginning of a clash of arms which must terminate one way or another.

Should our grave and learned philosophers find themselves overcome by this little three-legged spider, it will be mortifying; but in order to avoid that result, we fear they will have to do better than they have done yet.

On the other hand, before the Spiritualists can be allowed to claim the final victory in this contest, they should, it seems to me, be required to answer the following questions in a manner satisfactory to the highest intelligence and the better moral and religious sense of the community:

Why is it that "spirits" communicating through your mediums, by Planchette or otherwise, can not relate, plainly and circumstantially, *any* required incident of their lives, as a man would relate his history to a friend, instead of dealing so much in vague and ambiguous generalities, as they almost always do, and that, too, often in the bad grammar or bad spelling of the medium? Or, as a question allied to this, why is it that what purports to be the *same* spirit, generally, if not *always*, fails, when trial is made, to identify himself in the *same manner* through any two different mediums? Or, as another question still allied to the above, why is it that your Websters, Clays, Calhouns, and others, speaking through mediums, so universally give the idea that they have deteriorated in intellect since they passed into the spirit-world? And why is it that so little discourse or writing that possesses real merit, and so much that is mere drivel, has come through your mediums, if *spirits* are the authors? And why does it so often happen that the spirits—if they *are* spirits—can not communicate anything except what is already in the mind of the medium, or at least of some other person present? It does not quite answer these questions to say that the medium is "*undereloped*," unless you explain to us precisely on what principle the undevelopment affects the case. A speaking-trumpet may be "undeveloped"—cracked or wanting in some of its parts, so as to deteriorate the sound made through it; but we should at least expect that a man speaking through it would speak his own thoughts, and not the thoughts of the trumpet.

And then, looking at this subject in its *moral* and *social* aspects, the question should be answered: Why, on the supposition that these communications really come from immortal spirits, have they made so little progress, during the twenty years that they have been with us, in elevating the moral and social standard of human nature, in making better husbands and wives, parents and children, citizens and philanthropists, in drawing mankind together in harmony and charity, and founding and endowing great institutions for the elevation of the race? Rather may we not ask, in all kindness, why is it that the Spiritualist community has been little more than a Babel from the beginning to the present moment?

Or, ascending to the class of themes that come under the head of Religion: Why is it that prayer is so generally ignored, and the worship of God regarded as an unworthy superstition? Why is it that in the diatribes, dissertations, and speeches of those who profess to act under the sanction of the "spirits," we have a reproduction of so much of the slang and ribaldry of the infidels of the last century, and of the German Rationalism of the present, which is now being rejected by the Germans themselves? And why is it that in their references to the great lights of the world, we so often have Confucius, Jesus Christ, and William Shakspeare jumbled up into indistinguishability?

I do not say that all these questions may not be answered consistently with the claims of the spiritual hypothesis, but I *do* say that before our Spiritualist friends can have a *right* to expect the better portion of mankind to drink down this draft of philosophy which they have mixed, they must at least satisfy them that there is *no poison* in it.

Having thus exhibited these several theories, and, to an extent, discussed them *pro et contra*, it is but fair that we should now ask Planchette —using that name in a liberal sense—what is *her* theory of the whole matter? Perhaps it may be said that after raising this world of curiosity and doubt in the public mind as to its own origin and true nature, we have some semblance of a right to hold this mysterious intelligence responsible for a solution of the difficulty it has created; and perhaps if we are a little skillful in putting our questions, and occasionally call in the aid of Planchette's brothers and sisters, and other members of this mysterious family, we may obtain some satisfactory results.

PLANCHETTE'S OWN THEORY.

Planchette is intelligent; she can answer questions, and often answer them correctly, too. On what class of subjects, then, might she be expected to give answers more generally correct than those which relate to herself, especially if the questions be asked in a proper spirit, and under such conditions as are claimed to be requisite for correct responses? Following the suggestion of this thought, the original plan of this essay has been somewhat modified, and a careful consultation instituted, of which I here submit the results:

Inquirer. Planchette, excuse me if I now treat you as one on whom a little responsibility is supposed to rest. An exciter of curiosity, if as intelligent as you appear to be, should be able to satisfy curiosity; and a creator of doubts may be presumed to have some ability to solve doubts. May I not, then, expect from *you* a solution of the mysteries which have thus far enveloped you?

Planchette. That will depend much upon the spirit in which you may interrogate me, the pertinence of your questions, and your capacity to interpret the answers. If you propose a serious and careful consultation for really useful purposes, there is another thing which you should understand in the commencement. It is that, owing to conditions and laws which may yet be explained to you, I shall be compelled to use your own mind as a scaffolding, so to speak, on which to stand to pass you down the truths you may seek, and which are above the reach of your own mind alone. Keep your mind unperturbed, then, as well as intent upon your object, or I can do but little for you.

I. The question which stands as basic to all others which I wish to ask is, What is the nature of this power, intelligence, and will that communicates with us in this mysterious manner?

P. It is the reduplication of your own mental state; it is a spirit; it is the whole spiritual world; it is God—one or all, according to your condition and the form and aspect in which you are able to receive the communication.

I. That is covering rather too much ground for a beginning. For definiteness, suppose we take one of those points at a time. In saying, "It is a spirit," do you mean that you yourself, the immediate communicating agent, are an intelligence outside of, and separate from, myself, and that that intelligence is the spirit or soul of a man who once occupied a physical body, as I now do?

P. That is what I assert—only in reaffirmation of what the world, in explanation of similar phenomena, has been told a thousand times before.

I. Excuse me if I should question you a little closely on this point. There are grave difficulties in the way of an acceptance of this theory. The first of these is the *prima facie* absurdity of the idea.

P. Absurdity! How so?

I. It is so contrary to our ordinary course of thought; contrary, I may say, to our instincts; contrary to what the human faculties would naturally expect; contrary to the general experience of the world up to this time. In fact, the more highly educated minds of the world have long agreed in classing the idea as among the grossest of superstitions.

P. If you would, in place of each one of these assertions, affirm directly the contrary, you would come much nearer the truth. It is certain that the highest minds, as well as the lowest, of all ages and nations, with only such exceptions as prove rather than disprove the rule, have confidently believed in the occasional interposition of spirits in mundane affairs. True, there are in this age many of the class which you call the "more highly educated minds," who, spoiled by reasonings merely sensual, and hence necessarily sophistical, do not admit such an idea; but do not even these generally admit that there *is* an invisible world of spirits?

I. Most of them do; all professing Christians do. I do, certainly.

P. Let me test their consistency, and yours, then, by asking, Do they and you hold that one and the same God made all worlds, both natural and spiritual, and all things in them?

I. Of course they do; how otherwise?

P. Then, seeing that you acknowledge the unity of the Cause of all worlds and all things in them, you must acknowledge a certain union of all these in one universal system as the offspring of that one Cause, must you not?

I. Yes; I suppose the totality of things, natural and spiritual, must be acknowledged as forming, in some sense, one united system, of diverse but mutually correlated parts.

P. Please tell me, then, how there can be any united system in which the component parts, divisions, and subdivisions, down even to the most minute, are not each, necessarily and always, in communication with all the others, either immediately or mediately?

I. I see the point, and acknowledge it is ingeniously made; but do you not see that the argument fails to meet the whole difficulty?

P. What I do see is, that in admitting a connection of any kind, whether mediate or immediate, between the natural and spiritual worlds, you admit that a communication between the two worlds—hence between all things of one and all things of the other; hence between the intelligent inhabitants of one and those of the other—is logically not only possible but probable, not to say certain; and in this admission you yield the point under immediate discussion, and virtually concede that the idea of spirit-communication is not only *not absurd*, but is, indeed, among the most reasonable of things, to which ignorance and materialistic prejudice alone have given the aspect of absurdity.

I. Well, there is something in that which looks like argument, I must admit.

P. Can you not go a little farther and admit for established fact, proved by the testimony of the Book from which you derive your religious faith, that communications between spirits and mortals have sometimes taken place?

I. True, but the Bible calls the spirits thus communicating, " familiar spirits," and those who have dealings with them, " witches " and " wizards," and forbids the practice under severe penalties. How does that sound to you, my ingenious friend?

P. The way you put it, it sounds as though you did not quite understand the full scope of my question; but no matter, since it is at once a proof and an acknowledgment on your part that spirits have communicated with mortals—the essential point in dispute, which when once admitted will render further reasonings more plain. Let me ask you, however, was not the practice of consulting familiar spirits that is forbidden in the Bible, a practice that was common among the heathen nations of those times?

I. It was, and is spoken of as such in several passages.

P. Did not the heathens consult familiar spirits as petty divinities, or gods, and as such, follow their sayings and commands implicitly? and would not the Israelites to whom the Old Testament was addressed have violated the first command in the decalogue by adopting this practice? and was not that the reason, and the only reason, why the practice was forbidden?

I. To each of those questions I answer, Yes, certainly.

P. Do the Old or New Testament writings anywhere command us to abstain from all intercourse with spirits?—or from any intercourse which would not be a violation of the command, " Thou shalt have no other Gods before me?"

I. Really I do not know that the Bible contains any such command.

P. Do you not know, on the contrary, that spirits other than those called "familiar spirits," often did communicate, and with apparently good and legitimate purposes, too, with men whose names are mentioned in the Bible?

I. Well, I must in candor say that there were some cases of that kind.

P. May you not, then, from all this learn a rule which will always be a safe guide to you in respect to the matters under discussion? I submit for your consideration, that that rule is, "Be not forgetful to entertain strangers, for thereby some have entertained angels unawares." But even if the "strangers" that may come to you, either of your own world or the spirit-world, should prove to be "angels," do not follow them implicitly, or in an unreasoning manner, nor worship them as gods, for in so doing you would render yourself amenable to the law against having dealings with "familiar spirits."

I. I must admit that your remarks throw a somewhat new light on the subject, and I do not know that I can dispute what you say. But even admitting all your strong points thus far, the spirit-theory of Planchettism and other and kindred modern wonders remains encumbered with a mass of difficulties which it seems to me must be removed before it can be considered as having much claim to the credence of good and rational minds. On some of these points I propose now to question you somewhat closely, and shall hope that you will bear with me in the same patience and candor which you have thus far manifested.

P. Ask your questions, and I shall answer them to the best of my ability.

THE RATIONAL DIFFICULTY.

I. The difficulties, as they appear to me, are of a threefold character—*Rational*, *Moral*, and *Religious*. I begin with the first, the Rational Difficulty. And for a point to start from, let me ask, Is it true, as generally held, that when a man becomes disencumbered of the clogs and hinderances of the flesh, and passes into the spirit-world—especially into the realms of the just—his intellect becomes more clear and comprehensive?

P. That is true, as a general rule.

I. How is it, then, that in returning to communicate with us mortals, the alleged spirits of men who were great and wise while living on the earth, almost uniformly appear to have *degenerated* as to their mental faculties, being seldom, if ever, able to produce anything above mediocrity? And why is it that the speaking and writing purporting to come from spirits, are so generally in the bad grammar, bad spelling, and other distinctive peculiarities of the style of the medium, and so often express precisely what the medium knows, imagines, or surmises, and nothing more?

P. That your questions have a certain degree of pertinence, I must admit; but in making this estimate of the intelligence purporting to come from the spiritual world, have you not ignored some things which candor should have compelled you to take into the account? Think for a moment.

I. Well, perhaps I ought to have made an exception in your own favor. Your communication with me thus far has, I must admit, been characterized by a remarkable breadth and depth of intelligence, as well as ingenuity of argument.

P. And what, too, of the style and merits of the communications purporting to come from spirits to other persons and through other channels—are they not, as an almost universal rule, decidedly superior to anything the medium could produce unaided by the influence, whatever it may be, which acts upon him?

I. Perhaps they are; indeed, I must admit I have known many instances of alleged spirit-communications which, though evidently stamped with some of the characteristics of the medium, were quite above the normal capacity of the latter; yet in themselves considered, they were generally beneath the capacity of the *living man* from whose disembodied spirit they purported to come.

P. By just so much, then, as the production given through a medium is elevated above the medium's normal capacity, is the influence which acts upon him to be credited with the character of that production. Please make a note of this point gained. And now for the question why these communications should be tinctured with the characteristics of the medium at all; and why spirits can not, as a general rule, communicate to mortals their own normal intelligence, freely and without obstruction, as man communicates with man, or spirit with spirit. But that we may be enabled to make this mystery more clear, we had better attend first to another question which I see you have in your mind—the question as to the potential agent used by spirits in making communications.

THE MEDIUM—THE DOCTRINE OF SPHERES.

I. That is what we are anxious to understand; electricity, magnetism, odylic force, or whatever you may know or believe it to be—give us all the light you can on the subject.

P. Properly speaking, neither of these, or neither without important qualifications. Preparatory to the true explanation, I will lay the foundation of a new thought in your mind by asking, Do you know of any body or organism in nature—unless, indeed, it be a *dead* body—which has not something answering to an atmosphere?

I. It has been said by some astronomers that the moon has no atmosphere; though others, again, have expressed the opinion that she has, indeed, an atmosphere, but a very rare one.

P. Precisely so; and as might have been expected from the rarity of her atmosphere, she has the smallest amount of cosmic life of any planetary body in the solar system—only enough to admit of the smallest development of vegetable and animal forms. Still, every sun, planet, or other cosmic body in space is generally, and every regularly constituted form connected with that body is specifically, surrounded, and also pervaded, by its own peculiar and characteristic atmosphere; and to this universal rule, minerals, plants, animals, man, and in their own degree even the disembodied men whom you call " spirits," form no exception.

I. Do you mean to say that man and spirits, and also the lower living forms, are surrounded by a sphere of air or wind like the atmosphere of the earth, but yet no part of that atmosphere?

P. The atmospheres of other bodies than planets are not air or wind, but in their substances are so different from what you know as the atmospheres of planets as not to have anything specifically in common with them. The specific atmospheres of flowers, and when excited by friction, those also of some metals, and even of stone crystals, are often perceptible to the sense of smell, and are in that way distinguishable not only from the atmosphere of the earth, but also from the atmospheres of each other. But properly speaking, the psychic *aura* surrounding man and spirits should no longer be called an atmosphere, that is, an *atom-sphere* or sphere of atoms, but simply a " sphere;" for it is not atomic, that is, material, in its constitution, but is a spiritual substance, and as such extends indefinitely into space, or rather has only an indirect relation to space at all. Nor is the atmosphere, as popularly understood, the only enveloping sphere of the earth, for beyond and pervading it, and pervading also even all solid bodies, is a sublime interplanetary substance called " ether," the vehicle of light, and next approach to spiritual substance; while all bodies, solid, liquid, and gaseous, are also pervaded by electricity.

I. All that is interesting, but the subject is new to me, and I would like to have some further illustration. Can you cite me some familiar fact to prove that man is actually surrounded and pervaded by a sphere such as you describe?

P. I can only say that you are at times conscious of the fact yourself, as all persons are who are possessed of an ordinary degree of psychic sensitiveness. Does not even the silent presence of certain persons, though entire strangers, affect you with an uncomfortable sense of repulsion, perhaps embarrassing your thoughts and speech, while in the presence of others you at once feel perfectly free, easy, at home, and experience even a marked and mysterious sense of congeniality?

I. That is so; I have often noticed it, but never could account for it.

P. Farther than this, have you not at times when free from external disturbances, with the mind in a revery of loose thoughts, noticed the abrupt intrusion of the thought of a person altogether out of the line of your previous meditations, and then observed that the same person would come bodily into your presence very shortly afterward?

I. I have, frequently; the same phenomenon appears to have been noticed by others, and is so common an occurrence as to have given rise to the well-known slang proverb, "Speak of the devil and he will always appear."

P. Just so; but still further: Have you not personally known of instances, or been credibly informed of them, in which mutually sympathizing friends of highly sensitive organizations were mysteriously and correctly impressed with each other's general conditions, even when long distances apart, and without any external communication?

I. I have heard and read of many such cases, but could have scarcely believed them had I not had some experience of the kind myself.

P. There must, then, be here some medium of communication; that medium is evidently not anything cognizable to either of the five outer senses. What, then, can it be but the co-related spheres of the two persons, which I have already told you are not atomic—not material but spiritual, and as such have little relation to space?

I. That idea, if true, looks to me to be of some importance, and I would like you, if you can, to show me clearly what relation these "spheres," as you call them, have to the spiritual nature of man.

P. Consider, then, the primal meaning of the word "spirit:" It is derived from the Latin *spiritus*, the basic meaning of which is *breath*, *wind*, air—nearly the same idea that you attach to the word "atmosphere." So the Greek word *pneuma*, also translated "spirit," means precisely the same thing. The same meaning is likewise attached to the Hebrew word *ruach*, also sometimes translated "spirit." Now, carrying out this use of terms, the wind, air, or atmosphere of the earth (including the ether, electricity, and other imponderable elements) is the spirit of the earth;* the atmosphere of any other body, great or small, is the spirit of that body; the atmosphere, or rather sphere, being now without atoms, of a man, considered as an intellectual and moral being, is the spirit of that man; the sphere of a disembodied man or soul is the spirit of that man or soul; and so the Infinite and Eternal Sphere of the Deity which pervades and controls all creations both in the spiritual and natural universe, is the Spirit of the Deity, which in the Bible is called the Holy Spirit.

I. Well, those ideas seem singularly consistent with themselves, to say the least, however novel they may appear. But now another point: You have said that atmospheres or spheres surround and pervade all bodies, unless, indeed, they be *dead* bodies—attributing, as I understand you, a kind of *cosmic* life to plants, and a mineral life to minerals, as well as a vegetable and animal life respectively to vegetables and animals; do you mean by that to intimate that the sphere is the *effect* or the *cause* of the living body?

P. Of each living material form, the sphere, or at least *some* sphere, was the cause. Matter, considered simply by itself, is dead, and can only

---

* Query: Have we here the *spiritus mundi* of the old philosophers?

live by the influx of a surrounding sphere or spirit. It may be said at the last synthesis, that the *general* sphere even of each microscopic monad that is in process of becoming vitalized, as well as of the great nebulous mass that is to form a universe, is the Spirit of the Infinite Deity, which is present with atoms in the degree of atoms, as well as with worlds in the degree of worlds. This Spirit, as it embodies itself in matter, becomes segregated, finited, and individualized, and forms a specific soul, spirit, or sphere by itself, now no longer deific, but always of a nature necessarily corresponding to the peculiar form and condition of the matter in which it becomes embodied. Life, therefore, is not the result of organization, but organization is the result of life, which latter is eternal, never having had a beginning, and never to have an end. Some of your scientific men have recently discovered what they have been pleased to term "the physical basis of life," in a microscopic and faintly vital substance called *protoplasm*, which forms the material foundation of all organic structures, both in the vegetable and animal kingdoms. They have not yet, however, discovered the source from which the life found in this substance comes—which would be plain to them if they understood the doctrine of spheres and influx as I have here given it.

I. I thank you for this profoundly suggestive thought, even should it prove to be no more than a thought. But please now show us what bearing all this has upon the question more particularly before us—the question as to the medium and process through which this little board is moved, the tables are tipped, people are entranced and made to speak and write, and all these modern wonders are produced—also how and why it is that the alleged spirit-communications are commonly tinctured, more or less, with the peculiar characteristics of the human agents through whom they are given?

P. You now have some idea of the doctrine of spheres; you will, however, understand that the spheres of created beings, owing to a unity of origin, are universally co-related, and, under proper conditions, can act and react upon each other. You have before had some true notion of the laws of *rapport*, which means relation or correspondence. You will understand, further, that there can be no action between any two things or beings in any department of creation except as they are in *rapport* or correspondence with each other, and that the action can go no farther than the *rapport* or correspondence extends. Now, two spirits can always, when it is in divine order, readily communicate with each other, because they can always bring themselves into direct *rapport* at some one or more points. Though matter is widely discreted from spirit, in that the one is dead and the other is alive, yet there is a certain correspondence between the two, and between the degrees of one and the degrees of the other; and according to this correspondence, relation, or *rapport*, spirit may act upon matter. Thus your spirit, in all its degrees and faculties, is in the closest *rapport* with all the degrees of matter composing your body, and for this reason alone it is able to move it as it does, which it will no longer be able to do when that *rapport* is destroyed by what you call death. Through your body it is *en rapport* with, and is able to act upon, surrounding matter. If, then, you are in a susceptible condition, a spirit can not only get into *rapport* with your spirit, and through it with your body, and control its motions, or even suspend your own proper action and external consciousness by entrancement, but if you are at the same time *en rapport* with this little board, it can, through contact of your hands, get into *rapport* with *that*, and move it without any conscious or volitional agency on your part. Furthermore, under certain favorable conditions, a spirit may, through your sphere and body combined, come into *rapport* even with the spheres of the ultimate particles of material bodies near you, and thence with the particles and the whole bodies themselves, and may thus, even without contact of your hands, move them or make sounds upon them, as has often been witnessed. Its action, however, as before said, ceases where the *rapport* ceases; and if communications from really intelligent spirits have sometimes been defective as to the quality of the intelligence manifested, it is because there has been found nothing in the medium which could be brought into *rapport* or correspondence with the more elevated ideas of the spirit. The spirit, too, in frequent instances, is unable to prevent its energizing influences from being diverted by the reactive power of the medium, into the channels of the imperfect types of thought and expression that are established in his mind, and it is for this simple reason that the communication is, as you say, often tinctured with the peculiarities of the medium, and even sometimes is nothing more than a reproduction of the mental states of the latter, perhaps greatly intensified.

I. If this theory, so far seemingly very plausible, is really the correct one, it ought to go one step farther, and explain the many disorderly unintelligible rappings, thumpings, throwing of stones, hurling of furniture, etc., which often have occurred in the presence of particular persons, or at particular places.*

P. Those are manifestations which, when not the designed work of evil spirits, have their proximate source in the dream-region which lies between the natural and spiritual worlds.

I. Pray tell us what you mean by the dream-region that lies between the two worlds?

P. There are sometimes conditions in which the body is profoundly asleep, with no perturbations of the nervous system caused by previous mental and physical exercise. In this state the mind may still be perfectly awake, and independently, consciously, and even intensely active. When thus conditioned, it may be, and often is, among spirits in the

---

* See an article entitled "*A Remarkable Case of Physical Phenomena*," in the *Atlantic Monthly* for August, 1868.

spiritual world, though from the nature of the case it is seldom able to bring back into the bodily state any reminiscences of the scenes of that world. The dream state, properly speaking, is not this, but a state intermediate between this and the normal, wakeful state of the bodily senses, and is a state of broken, confused, irrational, inconsistent, and irresponsible thoughts, emotions, and apparent actions—the whole arising from confusedly intermixed bodily and spiritual states and influences. The potential spheres of spirits who desire to make manifestations to the natural world sometimes become commingled, designedly or otherwise, with the spheres of persons in the body who, in consequence of certain nervous or psychic disorders, are more or less in this dream-region even when the body is so far awake as to be *en rapport* with external things; and in such cases, whatever manifestations may arise from the spiritual potencies with which such persons are surcharged, will of necessity be beyond the control, or possibly even beyond the cognizance, of any governing spirit, and will be irrational, inconsistent, and sometimes very annoying, or even destructive, according to the types of the dreamy mentality of the medium. If you will think for a moment, you will remember that the kind of manifestations referred to are never known to occur except in the presence of persons in a semi-somnambulic or highly hysterical state, or laboring under some analogous nervous disorders; and the persons are often of a low organization, and very ignorant.

THE MORAL AND RELIGIOUS DIFFICULTY.

I. I am constrained to say, my mysterious friend, that the novelty and ingenuity of your ideas surprise me greatly, and I do, in all candor, acknowledge that you have skillfully disposed of my objections to the spiritual theory of these phenomena on *rational* grounds, and explained the philosophy of this thing, in a manner which I am at present unable to gainsay. I must still hesitate, however, to enroll myself among the converts to the spiritual theory unless you can remove another serious objection, which rests on *moral and religious grounds*. From so important and startling a development as general open communications from spirits, it seems to me that we would have a right to expect some conspicuous *good* to mankind; yet, although this thing has been before the world now over twenty years, I am unable to see the evidence that it has wrought any improvement in the moral and social condition of the converts to its claims. Pray, how do you account for that fact?

P. My friend, that question should be addressed to the Spiritualists, not to me. I will say, however, that this whole subject, long as it has been before the world, is still in a chaotic state, its laws have been very little understood, and even its essential objects and uses have been very much misconceived. I may add that, from its very nature, its real practical fruits as well as its true philosophy must necessarily be the growth of a considerable period of time.

I. I will not, then, press the objection in that form. When we look, however, at the *Religious* tendencies of the thing, I do not think we find much promise of the "practical fruits" which you here intimate may yet come of it. I lay it down as a proposition which all history proves, that Infidelity, in all its forms, is an enemy to the human race, and that it never has done or can do anybody any good, but always has done and must do harm. But it is notorious that the spirits, if they be such, with their mediums and disciples, have *generally* (though not universally, I grant) assumed an attitude at least of *apparent* hostility to almost every thing peculiar to the Christian religion, and most essential to it, and are constantly reiterating the almost identical ribaldry and sophistry of the infidels of the last century. How shall a good and Christian person who knows and has felt the truth of the vital principles of Christianity become a Spiritualist while Spiritualism thus denies and scoffs at doctrines which he *feels* and *knows* to be true?

P. The point you thus make is apparently a very strong one. But let me ask, Can you not conceive that there may be a difference between the mere word-teaching of Spiritualists and even spirits themselves, and the *real* teaching of Spiritualism as such? that is to say, between mere verbal utterances and phenomenal demonstrations? For illustration, suppose a man asserts at noonday that there is no sun, does he teach you there is no sun? or does he teach you that he is blind?

I. That he is blind, of course.

P. So, then, when a spirit comes to you and asserts that there is no God—it is seldom that they assert that, but we will take an extreme case —does he teach you that there is no God, or does he teach you that he himself is a fool?

I. Well, I should say he would teach the latter; but what use would the knowledge that he is such a fool be to us?

P. It is one of the important providential designs of these manifestations to teach mankind that spirits in general maintain the characters that they formed to themselves during their earthly life—that, indeed, they are the identical persons they were while dwelling in the flesh— hence, that while there are just, truthful, wise, and Christian spirits, there are also spirits addicted to lying, profanity, obscenity, mischief, and violence, and spirits who deny God and religion, just as they did while in your world. It has become very necessary for mankind to know all this; it certainly could in no other way be so effectually made known as by an actual manifestation of it; and it is just as necessary that you should see the *dark* side as the *bright* side of the picture.

I. Yet a person already adopting, or predisposed to adopt, any false doctrine asserted by a spirit, would, it seems to me, be in danger of receiving the spirit-assertion as *verbally* true.

P. That is to say, a person already in, or inclined to adopt, the same error that a spirit is in, would be in danger of being confirmed, for the time being, in that error, by listening to the spirit's asseveration. This, I admit, is just the effect produced for a time by the infidel word-teaching of some spirits upon those *already* embracing, or inclined to embrace, infidel sentiments. But if you will look beyond this superficial aspect of the subject at its great phenomenal and rational teachings, I think you will see that its deeper, stronger, and more permanent tendency is, not to promote infidelity, but ultimately to destroy it for ever. I have said before, that the real object of this development has been very much misconceived; I tell you now that the great object is to purge the Church itself of its latent infidelity; to renovate the Christian faith; and to bring theology and religion up to that high standard which will be equal to the wants of this age, as it certainly now is not.

I. Planchette, you are now touching upon a delicate subject. You should know that we are inclined to be somewhat tenacious of our theological and religious sentiments, and not to look with favor on any innovations. Nevertheless, I am curious to know how you justify yourself in this disparaging remark on the theology and religion of the day?

P. I do not mean to be understood that there is not much that is true and good in it. There is; and I would not by a single harsh word wound the loving hearts of those who have a spark of real religious life in them. I would bind up the bruised reed, rather than break it; I would fan the smoking flax into a flame, rather than quench it. This is the sentiment of all *good* spirits, of whom I trust I am one. But let me say most emphatically, that you want a public religion that will tower high above all other influences whatsoever; that will predominate over all, and ask favors of none; that will unite mankind in charity and brotherly love, and not divide them into hostile sects, and that will infuse its spirit into, and thus give direction to, all social and political movements. Such a religion the world must have, or from this hour degenerate.

I. Why might not the religion of the existing churches accomplish these results, provided its professors would manifest the requisite zeal and energy?

P. It is doing much good, and might, on the conditions you specify, do much more. Yet the public religion has become negative to other influences, instead of positive, as it should be, from which false position it can not be reclaimed without such great and vital improvements as would almost seem to amount to a renewal *ab ovo*.

I. On what ground do you assert that the religion of the day stands in a position "negative" to other influences?

P. I will answer by asking: Is it not patent to you and all other intelligent persons, that for the last hundred years the Christian Church and theology have been standing mainly on the defensive against the assaults of materialism and the encroachments of science? Has it not, without adequate examination, poured contempt on Mesmerism, denounced Phrenology, endeavored to explain away the facts of Geology and some of the higher branches of Astronomy? Has it not looked with a jealous eye upon the progress of science generally? and has it not been at infinite labor in merely defending the *history* of the life, miracles, death, and resurrection of Christ, against the negations of materialists, which labor might, in a great measure, have been saved if an adequate proof could have been given of the power and omnipotent working of a *present* Christ? And what is the course it has taken with reference to the present spiritual manifestations, the claims of which it can no more overthrow than it can drag the sun from the firmament? Now a true church—a church to which is given the power to cast out devils, and take up serpents, or drink any deadly thing, without being harmed—will always be able to stand on the aggressive against its *real* spiritual foes more than on the mere defensive, and in no case will it ever turn its back to a fact in science. Its power will be the power of the Holy Spirit, and not the power of worldly wealth and fashion. When it reasons of righteousness, temperance, and judgment, Felix will tremble, but it will never tremble before Felix, lest he withdraw his patronage from it.

I. I admit that the facts you state about the Church's warfare in these latter days have not the most favorable aspect; but how the needed elements of theology and religion are to be supplied by demonstrations afforded by these latter-day phenomena, I do not yet quite see.

P. If religious teachers will but study these facts, simply *as* facts, in all the different aspects which they have presented, from their first appearance up to this time—study them in the same spirit in which the chemist studies affinities, equivalents, and isomeric compounds—in the same spirit in which the astronomer observes planets, suns, and nebulæ— in the same spirit in which the microscopist studies monads, blood-discs, and protoplasm—always hospitable to a new fact, always willing to give up an old error for the sake of a new truth; never receiving the mere *dicta* either of spirits or men as absolute authority, but always trusting the guidance of right reason wherever she may lead—if, I say, they will but study these great latter-day signs, providential warnings and monitions, in this spirit, I promise them that they shall soon find a *rational* and *scientific* ground on which to rest every real Christian doctrine, from the Incarnation to the crown of glory—miracles, the regeneration, the resurrection, and all, with the great advantage of having the doctrine of immortality taken out of the sphere of *faith* and made a *fixed fact.* Furthermore, I promise them, on these conditions, that they shall hereafter be able to *lead* science rather than be dragged along unwillingly in its trail; and then science will be forever enrolled in the service of God's religion, and no longer in that of the world's materialism and infidelity.

I. Planchette, your communication has, upon the whole, been of a most startling character; tell me, I pray you, what do you call all this thing, and what is to come of it?

WHAT THIS MODERN DEVELOPMENT IS, AND WHAT IS TO COME OF IT.

P. Can you, then, bear an announcement still more startling than any I have yet made?

I. I really know not; I will try; let us have it.

P. Well, then, I call it a Fourth Great Divine Epiphany or Manifestation; or what you will perhaps better understand as one of the developments characterizing the beginning of a Fourth Great Divine Dispensation. What is to come of it, you will be able to judge as well as I when you understand its nature.

I. What! so great an event heralded by so questionable an instrumentality as the rapping and table tipping spirits?

P. Be calm, and at the same time be humble. Remember that it is not unusual for God to employ the foolish things of this world to confound the wise, and that when He comes to visit His people, He almost always comes in disguises, and sometimes even "as a thief in the night." Besides the spirits of which you speak are only the rough but very useful pioneers to open a highway through which the King is coming with innumerable hosts of angels, who, indeed, are already near you, though you see them not. It is, indeed, an hour of temptation that has come upon all the world; but be watchful and true, prayerful and faithful, and fear not.

I. Please tell us then, if you can, something of the nature and objects of this new Divine Epiphany which you announce; and as you say it is a *Fourth*, please tell us, in brief, what were the preceding *Three*, the times of their occurrence, and how they are all distinguished from each other.

P. The *First* appealed only to the affections and the inner sense of the soul, and was the Dispensation of the most ancient Church, when God walked with man in the midst of the garden of his own interior delights, and when "Enoch walked with God and was not, for God took him." But as this sense of the indwelling presence of God was little more than a mere *emotion*, for which, in that period of humanity's childhood, there was no adequate, rational, and directive intelligence, men, in process of time, began to mistake *every* delight as being divine and holy; thus they justified themselves in their *evil* delights, or in the gratification of their lusts and passions, considering even these as all divine. [The "sons of God" marrying the "daughters of men."—*Gen.* vi. 2–4.] And as they possessed no adequate reasoning faculty to which appeals might be made for the correction of these tendencies, and thus no ground of reformation, the race gradually grew to such a towering height of wickedness that it had to be almost entirely destroyed. The *Second* age or Dispensation, commencing with Noah, was distinctively characterized by the more special manifestation of God in outward types and shadows, in the *adyta* of temples and other consecrated places and things, from which, as representative seats of the Divine Presence, and through inspired men, were issued *law*, to which terrible penalties were annexed, as is exemplified by the law issued from Mount Sinai. The evil passions of men were thus put under restraint, and a rational faculty of discriminating between right and wrong—that is to say, a *Conscience*—was at the same time developed. But the sophistical use of these types and shadows (of which all ancient mythology is an outgrowth), and the accompanying perversion of the general conscience of mankind, gradually generated *Idolatry* and *Magic* with all their complicated evils, against which the Jewish Church, though belonging to the same general Dispensation, was specially instituted to react. Furthermore, as the mere restraints of penal law necessarily imply the existence in man of latent evils upon which the restraint is imposed, it is manifest that such a dispensation alone could not bring human nature to a state of perfection; and so a *Third* was instituted, in which *God was manifested in the flesh*. That is to say, He became incarnate in one man who was so constituted as to embody in himself the qualitative totality of Human Nature, that through this one Man as the Head of the Body of which other men were the subordinate organs, He might become united with all others—so that by the spontaneous movings of the living Christ within, and thus in perfect freedom, they might live the divine life in their very fleshly nature, previously the source of all sinful lusts, but now, together with the inner man, wholly regenerated and made anew. Here, then, is a *Trinity* of Divine manifestations, to the corresponding triune degrees of the nature of man—the inner or affectional degree, the intermediate, rational, or conscience degree, and the external, or sensuous degree.

But while this was all that was necessary as a ground for the perfect union of man with God, in the graduated triune degrees here mentioned, and thus all that was necessary for his personal salvation in a sphere of being beyond and above the earthy, it was *not* all that was necessary to perfect his relations to the great and mysterious realm of forms, materials, and forces which constitute the theater of his earthly struggles; nor was it quite all that was necessary to project and carry into execution the plan of that true and divine structure, order and government of human society which might be appropriately termed "the kingdom of heaven upon earth; wherefore you have now, according to a divine promise frequently repeated in the New Testament, a *Fourth* Great Divine Manifestation, which proves to be a manifestation of God in *universal science*.

I. But that "*Fourth* Manifestation" (or "*second* coming," as we are in the habit of calling it), which was promised in the New Testament, was to be attended with imposing phenomena, of which we have as yet seen nothing. It was to be a coming of Christ "in the clouds of heaven, with power and great glory," and the resurrection of the dead, the final judgment, etc., were to occur at the same time?

P. Certainly; but you would not, of course, insist upon putting a strictly literal interpretation upon this language, and thus turning it into utter and senseless absurdity. The *real* "*heaven*" is not that boundary of your vision in upper space which you call the sky, but the interior and living reality of things. The "*clouds*" that are meant are not those sheets of condensed aqueous vapor which float above your head, but the material coatings which have hitherto obscured interior realities, and through which the Divine *Logos*, the "Sun of Righteousness," is now breaking with a "power" which moves dead matter without visible hands, and with a "great glory," or light, which reveals a spiritual world within the natural. The "*Resurrection*" is not the opening of the literal graves, and re-assembling of the identical flesh, blood, and bones of dead men and nations which, during hundreds and even thousands of years, have been combining and re-combining with the universal elements; but it is the re-establishment of the long-suspended relations of spirits with the earthly sphere of being, by which they are enabled to freely manifest themselves again to their friends in the earthly life, and often to receive great benefits in return; and if you do not yet see, as accompanying and growing out of all this, the beginning of an ordeal that is to try souls, institutions, creeds, churches, and nations, as by fire, you had better wait awhile for a more full exposition of the "*last judgment*." People should learn that the kingdom of God comes not to *outward* but to *inward* observation, and that as for the prophetic words which have been spoken on this subject, "they are spirit, and they are life."

I. And what of the changed aspects of science that is to grow out of this alleged peculiar Divine manifestation?

P. To answer that question fully would require volumes. Be content, then, for the present, with the following brief words: Hitherto science has been almost wholly materialistic in its tendencies, having nothing to do with spiritual things, but ignoring and casting doubts upon them; while *spiritual* matters, on the other hand, have been regarded by the Church wholly as matters of faith with which science has nothing to do. But through these modern manifestations, God is providentially furnishing to the world all the elements of a spiritual science which, when established and recognized, will be the stand-point from which all physical science will be viewed. It will then be more distinctly known that all external and visible forms and motions originate from invisible, spiritual, and ultimately divine causes; that between cause and effect there is always a necessary and intimate *correspondence;* and hence that the whole outer universe is but the symbol and sure index of an invisible and *vastly more real* universe within. From this unitary basis of thought the different sciences as now correctly understood may be co-related in harmonic order as One Grand Science, the *known* of which, by the rule of correspondence, will lead by easy clews to the *unknown*. The true structure and government of human society will be clearly hinted by the structure and laws of the universe, and especially by that *microcosm*, or little universe, the human organization. All the great stirring questions of the day, including the questions of suffrage, woman's rights, the relations between labor and capital, and the questions of general political reform, will be put into the way of an easy and speedy solution; and mankind will be ushered into the light of a brighter day, socially, politically, and religiously, than has ever yet dawned upon the world.

I. My invisible friend, the wonderful nature of your communication excites my curiosity to know your name ere we part. Will you have the kindness to gratify me in this particular?

P. That I may not do. My name is of no consequence in any respect. Besides, if I should give it, you might, unconsciously to yourself, be influenced to attach to it the weight of a personal authority, which is specially to be avoided in communications of this kind. There is nothing to prevent deceiving spirits from assuming great names, and you have no way of holding them responsible for their statements. With thinkers—minds that are developed to a vigorous maturity—the truth itself should be its only and sufficient authority. If what I have told you appears intrinsically rational, logical, scientific, in harmony with known facts, and appeals to your convictions with the force of truth, accept it; if not, reject it; but I advise you not to reject it before giving it a candid and careful examination. I may tell you more at some future time, but for the present, farewell.

CONCLUSION.

Here the interview ended. It was a part of my original plan, after reviewing various theories on this mysterious subject, to propound one of my own; but this interview with Planchette has changed my mind. I confess I am amazed and confounded, and have nothing to say. The commendable motive which the invisible intelligence, whatever it may be, assigned in the last paragraph for refusing to give its name, also prompts me to withhold my own name from this publication for the present, and likewise to abstain from the explanation I intended to give of certain particulars as to the manner and circumstances of this communication. On its own intrinsic merits alone it should be permitted to rest; and as I certainly feel that my own conceptions have been greatly enlarged, not to say that I have been greatly instructed, I give it forth in the hope that it may have the same effect upon my readers.

HOW TO WORK PLANCHETTE.

WE have received letters from different persons who have tried Planchette, but failed to make her work. Our correspondents wish to know the reason of the failure, and what conditions must be complied with on their part to remedy the difficulty. We reply by the insertion of the following rules, which should be read in connection with the descriptive paragraph near the commencement of this pamphlet:

RULES TO BE OBSERVED IN USING PLANCHETTE.

For some persons (strong magnetizers), "Planchette" moves at once, and for one such person it moves rapidly and writes distinctly. With such a person it is not necessary for another to put their hands on; it will operate alone for them, and better than with two persons.

It has been noticed that one pair of male and one pair of female hands form a more perfect Battery to work "Planchette" than two males or two females would do.

It has also been noticed that one light and one dark complexioned person are better than two light or two dark persons would be together; also, that two females, with their hands on together, are better than the hands of two males would be.

If, after observing these rules, "Planchette" should refuse to write, or move, different persons must try until the necessary Battery is formed to make it operate. (It is here remarked that the average number of persons able to work "Planchette" is about five to eight; but it is still possible, but improbable, to have an assemblage of eight persons and not any be able to make "Planchette" go.) After it is ascertained who are the proper persons to move "Planchette," no end of fun, amusement, and possibly instruction, will be afforded.

According to the experience of the present writer, the proportional number of those for whom Planchette will work promptly, and from the first, is not quite so great as here given. But by perseverance through repeated trials, under the right mental and physical conditions, most persons may at length obtain responsive movements, more or less satisfactory. Planchette, however (or the intelligence which moves her), likes to be treated with a decent respect, and has a repugnance to confusion. Ask her, therefore, none but respectful questions, and *only one of these at a time;* and when there are several persons in the company anxious to obtain responses, while one is consulting let all the others keep *perfectly quiet*, and each patiently await his turn. A noncompliance with these conditions generally spoils the experiment.

SPIRITUALISM.

BY MRS. HARRIET BEECHER STOWE.

[The following was written for, and published in the *Christian Union*. It was reprinted in THE PHRENOLOGICAL JOURNAL in 1870. We present it here, as in some measure explanatory of all the matter which precedes it. There are many who do not accept all that is claimed to be true, in Modern Spiritualism, who will entertain the moderate views expressed by The Author of Uncle Tom's Cabin. EDITOR.]

IT is claimed that there are in the United States four million Spiritualists. The perusal of the advertisements in any one of the weekly newspapers devoted to this subject will show that there is a system organized all over the Union to spread these sentiments. From fifty to a hundred, and sometimes more, of lecturers advertise in a single paper, to speak up and down the land; and lyceums—progressive lyceums for children, spiritual pic-nics, and other movements of the same kind, are advertised. This kind of thing has been going on from year to year, and the indications now are that it is increasing rather than diminishing.

It is claimed by the advocates of these sentiments that the number of those who boldly and openly profess them is exceeded by the greater number of those who are *secretly* convinced, but who are unwilling to encounter the degree of obloquy or ridicule which they would probably meet on an open avowal.

All these things afford matter for grave thought to those to whom none of the great and deep movements of society are indifferent. When we think how very tender and sacred are the feelings with which this has to do—what power and permanency they always must have, we can not but consider such a movement of society entitled at least to the most serious and thoughtful consideration.

Our own country has just been plowed and seamed by a cruel war. The bullet that has pierced thousands of faithful breasts has cut the nerve of life and hope in thousands of homes. What yearning toward the invisible state, what agonized longings must have gone up as the sound of mournful surges, during these years succeeding the war! Can we wonder that any form of religion, or of superstition, which professes in the least to mitigate the anguish of that cruel separation, and to break that dreadful silence by any voice or token, has hundreds of thousands of disciples? If on review of the spiritualistic papers and pamphlets we find them full of vague wanderings and wild and purposeless flights of fancy, can we help pitying that craving of the human soul which all this represents and so imperfectly supplies?

The question arises, Has not the Protestant religion neglected to provide some portion of the true spiritual food of the human soul, and thus produced this epidemic craving? It is often held to be a medical fact that morbid appetites are the blind cry of nature for something needed in the bodily system which is lacking. The wise nurse or mother does not hold up to ridicule the poor little culprit who secretly picks a hole in the plastering that he may eat the lime; she considers within herself what is wanting in this little one's system, and how this lack shall be more judiciously and safely supplied. If it be phosphate of lime for the bones which nature is thus blindly crying for, let us give it to him more palatab'y and under more attractive forms.

So with the epidemic cravings of human society. The wise spiritual pastor or master would inquire what is wanting to these poor souls that they are thus with hungry avidity rushing in a certain direction, and devouring with unhealthy eagerness all manner of crudities and absurdities.

May it not be spiritual food, of which their mother, the Church, has abundance, which she has neglected to set before them?

Now, if we compare the religious teachings of the present century with those of any past one, we shall find that the practical spiritualistic belief taught by the Bible has to a great extent dropped out of it.

Let us begin with the time of Jesus Christ. Nothing is more evident in reading his life than that he was acting all the time in view of *unseen* and spiritual influences, which were more pronounced and operative to him than any of the *visible* and materialistic phenomena of the present life. In this respect the conduct of Christ, if imitated in the present day, would subject a man to the imputation of superstition or credulity. He imputed things to the direct agency of invisible spirits acting in the affairs of life, that we, in the same circumstances, attribute only to the constitutional liabilities of the individual acted upon by force of circumstances.

As an example of this, let us take his language toward the Apostle Peter. With the habits of modern Christianity, the caution of Christ to Peter would have been expressed much on this fashion: "Simon, Simon, thou art impulsive, and liable to be carried away with sudden impressions. The Jews are about to make an attack on me which will endanger thee."

This was the exterior view of the situation, but our Lord did not take it. He said, "Simon, Simon, Satan hath desired to have thee that he may sift thee as wheat; but I have prayed for thee, that thy faith fail not." This Satan was a person ever present in the mind of Christ. He was ever in his view as the invisible force by which all the visible antagonistic forces were ruled. When his disciples came home in triumph to relate the successes of their first preaching tour, Christ said, " I beheld Satan as lightning fall from heaven." When the Apostle Peter rebuked him for prophesying the tragical end of his earthly career, Christ answered not him, but the invisible spirit whose influence over him he recognized: " Get thee behind me, Satan ! Thou art an offense unto me."

When the Saviour's last trial approached, he announced the coming crisis in the words, " The prince of this world cometh, and hath nothing in me." When he gave himself into the hands of the Sanhedrim, he said," This is your hour and that of the powers of darkness." When disputing with the unbelieving Jews, he told them that they were of their father, the devil ; that he was a murderer from the beginning, and abode not in the truth ; that when he spoke a lie he spoke of his own, for he was a liar, and the father of lies.

In short, the life of Christ, as viewed by himself, was not a conflict with enemies *in the flesh*, but with an invisible enemy, artful, powerful, old as the foundations of the world, and ruling by his influences over evil spirits and men in the flesh.

The same was the doctrine taught by the Apostles. In reading the Epistles we see in the strongest language how the whole visible world was up in arms against them. St. Paul gives this catalogue of his physical and worldly sufferings, proving his right to apostleship mainly by perseverance in persecution. " In labors more abundant, in stripes above measure, in prisons more frequent, in deaths oft; of the Jews five times received I forty stripes save one ; thrice was I beaten with rods, once was I stoned ; thrice have I suffered shipwreck—a night and a day have I been in the deep. In journeyings often, in perils of water, in perils of robbers, in perils by mine own countrymen, in perils by the heathen, in perils in the city, in perils in the wilderness, in perils among false brethren."

One would say with all this, there was a sufficient array of physical and natural causes against St. Paul to stand for something. In modern language — yea, in the language of good modern Christians—it would be said " What is the use of taking into account any devil or any invisible spirits to account for Paul's trials and difficulties ?—it is enough that the whole world has set itself against what he teaches—Jew and Gentile are equally antagonistic to it."

But St. Paul says in the face of all this, " We are not wrestling with flesh and blood, but with principalities and powers and the leaders of the darkness of this world, and against wicked spirits in high places ;" and St. Peter, recognizing the sufferings and persecutions of the early Christians, says, " Be sober, be vigilant." Why ? " Because your adversary, the devil, as a roaring lion, goeth about seeking whom he may devour."

In like manner we find in the discourses of our Lord and the Apostles the recognition of a counteracting force of good spirits. When Nathaniel, one of his early disciples, was astonished at his spiritual insight, he said to him, "Thou shalt see greater things than these! Hereafter ye shall see heaven open, and angels of God ascending and descending on the Son of man." When he spoke of the importance of little children, he announced that each one of them had a guardian angel who beheld the face of God. When he was transfigured on the Mount, Moses and Elijah appeared in glory, and talked with him of his death that he was to accomplish at Jerusalem. In the hour of his agony in the garden, an angel appeared and ministered to him. When Peter drew a sword to defend him, he said, "Put up thy sword. Thinkest thou that I can not now pray to my Father, and he will give me more than twelve legions of angels?"

Thus, between two contending forces of the invisible world was Christianity inaugurated. During the primitive ages the same language was used by the Fathers of the church, and has ever since been traditional.

But we need not say that the fashion of modern Protestant theology and the custom of modern Prostestant Christianity have been less and less of this sort.

We hear from good Christians, and from Christian ministers, talk of this sort: A great deal is laid to the poor devil that he never thought of. If men would take care of their own affairs the devil will let them alone. We hear it said that there is no *evidence* of the operation of invisible spirits in the course of human affairs. It is all a mere matter of physical, mental, and moral laws working out their mission with unvarying certainty.

But is it a fact, then, that the great enemy whom Christ so constantly spoke of is dead? Are the principalities and powers and rulers of the darkness of this world, whom Paul declared to be the real opponents that the Christian has to arm against, all dead? If that great enemy whom Christ declared the source of all opposition to himself is yet living, with his nature unchanged, there is as much reason to look for his action behind the actions of men and the vail of material causes as there was in Christ's time; and if the principalities and powers and rulers of the darkness of this world, that Paul speaks of, have not died, then they are now, as they were in his day, the *principal* thing the Christian should keep in mind and against which he should arm.

And, on the other hand, if it is true, as Christ declared, that every little child in him has a guardian angel, who always beholds the Father's face; if, as St. Paul says, it is true that the angels all are " ministering spirits sent forth to minister to those who shall be heirs of salvation," then it follows that every one of us is being constantly watched over, cared for, warned, guided, and ministered to by invisible spirits.

Now let us notice in what regions and in what classes of mind the modern spiritualistic religion has most converts.

To a remarkable degree it takes minds which have been denuded of all faith in spirits; minds which are empty, swept of all spiritual belief, are the ones into which any amount of spirits can enter and take possession.

That is to say, the human soul, in a state of starvation for one of its normal and most necessary articles of food, devours right and left every marvel of modern spiritualism, however crude.

The old angelology of the Book of Daniel and the Revelation is poetical and grand. Daniel sees lofty visions of beings embodying all the grand forces of nature. He is told of invisible princes who rule the destiny of nations! Michael, the guardian prince of the Jews, is hindered twenty-one days from coming, at the prayer of Daniel, by the conflicting princes of Media and Persia. In the New Testament, how splendid is the description of the angel of the resurrection! "And behold, there was a great earthquake, and the angel of the Lord descended from heaven and came and rolled back the stone from the door and sat upon it! His countenance was as the lightning, and his raiment white as snow, and for fear of him the keepers did shake and become as dead men." We have here spiritualistic phenomena worthy of a God—worthy our highest conceptions—elevated, poetic, mysterious, grand!

And communities, and systems of philosophy and theology, which have explained all the supernatural art of the Bible, or which are always apologizing for it, blushing for it, ignoring and making the least they can of it—such communities will go into spiritualism by hundreds and by thousands. Instead of angels, whose countenance is as the lightning, they will have ghosts and tippings and tappings and rappings. Instead of the great beneficent miracles recorded in Scripture, they will have senseless clatterings of furniture and breaking of crockery. Instead of Christ's own promise, "He that keepeth my commandments, I will love him and manifest *myself*," they will have manifestations from all sorts of anonymous spirits, good, bad, and indifferent.

Well, then, what is the way to deal with spiritualism? Precisely what the hunter uses when he stands in the high, combustible grass and sees the fire sweeping around him on the prairies. He sets fire to the grass all around him, and it burns *from* instead of *to* him, and thus he fights fire with fire. Spiritualism, in its crudities and errors, can be met only in that way. The true spiritualism of the Bible is what will be the only remedy for the cravings of that which is false and delusive.

Some years ago the writer of this, in deep sorrow for the sudden death of a son, received the following letter from a Roman Catholic priest, in a neighboring town. He was a man eminent for holiness of life and benevolence, and has since entered the rest of the blessed.

DEAR MADAM: In the deep affliction that has recently visited you I implore you to remember well that there is a communion of spirits of the departed just, which death can not prevent, and which, with prayer, can impart much consolation. This, with the condolence of every parent and child in my flock, I beg leave to offer you, wishing, in the mean time, to assure you of my heartfelt regret and sympathy.

Yours, very truly, JAMES O'DONNELL,
Catholic Pastor, Lawrence.

What is this communion which death can not prevent, and which with prayer can impart consolation? It is known in the Apostles' Creed as

"THE COMMUNION OF SAINTS."

When it is considered what social penalties attach to the profession of this faith, one must admit that only some very strong cause can induce persons of standing and established reputation openly to express beliefs of this kind. The penalty is loss of confidence and being reputed of unsound mind. It is not an easy thing to profess belief in anything which destroys one's reputation for sanity, yet undoubtedly this is the result.

It must also be admitted that most of the literature which has come into existence in this way is of a doubtful and disreputable kind, and of a tendency to degrade rather than elevate our conceptions of a spiritual state.

Yet such is the hunger, the longing, the wild craving of the human soul for the region of future immortality, its home-sickness for its future home, its perishing anguish of desire for the beloved ones who have been torn away from it, and to whom in every nerve it still throbs and bleeds, that professed words and messages from that state, however unworthy, are met with a trembling agony of eagerness, a willingness to be deceived, most sorrowful to witness.

But any one who judges of the force of this temptation merely by what is published in the *Banner of Light*, and other papers of that class, has little estimate of what there is to be considered in the way of existing phenomena under this head.

The cold scientists who, without pity and without sympathy, have supposed that they have had under their dissecting knives the very phenomena which have deluded their fellows, mistake. They have not seen them, and in the cold, unsympathizing mood of science, they never can see them. The experiences that have most weight with multitudes who believe more than they dare to utter, are secrets deep as the grave, sacred as the innermost fibers of their souls—they can not bring their voices to utter them except in some hour of uttermost confidence and to some friend of tried sympathy. They know what they have seen and what they have heard. They know the examinations they have made they know the inexplicable results, and, like Mary of old, they keep all these sayings and ponder them in their hearts. They have no sympathy with the vulgar, noisy, outward phenomena of tippings and rappings and signs and wonders. They have no sympathy with the vulgar and profane attacks on the Bible, which form part of the utterances of modern seers; but they can not forget, and they can not explain things which in sacred solitude or under circumstances of careful observation have come under their own notice. They have no wish to make converts—they shrink from conversation, they wait for light; but, when they hear all these things scoffed at, they think within themselves—Who knows?

We have said that the strong, unregulated, and often false spiritualistic current of to-day is a result of the gradual departure of Christendom from the true supernaturalism of primitive ages. We have shown how Christ and his Apostles always regarded the invisible actors on the stage of human existence as more powerful than the visible ones; that they referred to their influence over the human spirit and over the forces of nature, things which modern rationalism refers only to natural laws. We can not illustrate the departure of modern society from primitive faith better than in a single instance—a striking one.

The Apostles' Creed is the best formula of Christian faith—it is common to the Greek, the Roman, the Reformed Churches, and published by our Pilgrim Fathers in the New England Primer in connection with the Assembly's Catechism. It contains the following profession:

"I believe in the Holy Ghost; the Holy Catholic Church; the Communion of Saints; the Forgiveness of Sins," etc.

In this sentence, according to Bishop Pearson on the Creed, are announced four important doctrines: 1. The Holy Ghost; 2. The Holy Catholic Church; 3. The Communion of Saints; 4. The Forgiveness of Sins.

To each one of these the good Bishop devotes some twenty or thirty pages of explanation.

But it is customary with many clergymen in reading to slur the second and third articles together, thus: "I believe in the Holy Catholic Church, the communion of saints"—that is to say, I believe in the Holy Catholic Church, which is the communion of saints.

Now, in the standard edition of the English Prayer Book, and in all the editions published from it, the separate articles of faith are divided by semicolons—thus: "The Holy Ghost; The Holy Catholic Church; The Communion of Saints." But in our American editions the punctuation is altered to suit a modern rationalistic idea—thus: "The Holy Catholic Church, the Communion of Saints."

The doctrine of the Communion of Saints, as held by primitive Christians, and held still by the Roman and Greek Churches, is thus dropped out of view in the modern Protestant Episcopal reading.

But what is this doctrine? Bishop Pearson devotes a long essay to it, ending thus:

Every one may learn by this what he is to understand by this part of the article in which he professeth to believe in the Communion of Saints.

Thereby he is conceived to express thus much:

"I am fully persuaded of this, as a necessary and infallible truth, that such persons as are truly sanctified in the Church of Christ, while they live in the crooked generations of men and struggle with all the miseries of this world, have fellowship with God the Father, God the Son, and God the Holy Ghost . . . . . . that they partake of the kindness and care of the blessed angels who take delight in ministrations for their benefit, that . . . . . . they have an intimate union and conjunction with all the saints on earth as being members of Christ; NOR IS THIS UNION SEPARATED BY THE DEATH OF ANY, but they have communion with all the saints who, from the death of Abel, have departed this life in the fear of God, and now enjoy the presence of the Father, and follow the Lamb whithersoever he goeth.

"*And thus I believe in the Communion of Saints.*"

Now, we appeal to the consciences of modern Christians whether this statement of the doctrine of the Communion of Saints represents the doctrine that they have heard preached from the pulpit, and whether it has been made practically so much the food and nourishment of their souls as to give them all the support under affliction and bereavement which it certainly is calculated to do?

Do they really believe themselves to partake in their life-struggle of the kindness and care of the blessed angels who take delight in ministrations for their benefit? Do they believe they are united by intimate bonds with all Christ's followers? Do they believe that the union is not separated by the death of any of them, but that they have communion with all the saints who have departed this life in the faith and now enjoy the presence of the Father?

Would not a sermon conceived in the terms of this standard treatise excite an instant sensation as tending toward the errors of Spiritualism? And let us recollect that the Apostles' Creed from which this is taken was as much a standard with our Pilgrim Fathers as the Cambridge Platform.

If we look back to Cotton Mather's Magnalia, we shall find that the belief in the ministration of angels and the conflict of invisible spirits, good and evil, in the affairs of men, was practical and influential in the times of our fathers.

If we look at the first New England Systematic Theology, that of Dr. Dwight, we shall find the subject of Angels and Devils and their ministry among men fully considered.

In the present theological course at Andover that subject is wholly omitted. What may be the custom in other theological seminaries of the present day we will not say.

We will now show what the teaching and the feeling of the primitive church was on the subject of the departed dead and the ministrations of angels. In *Coleman's Christian Antiquities*, under the head of Death and Burial of the Early Christians, we find evidence of the great and wide difference which existed between the Christian community and all the other world, whether Jews or heathen, in regard to the vividness of their conceptions of immortality. The Christian who died was not counted as lost from their number—the fellowship with him was still unbroken. The theory and the practice of the Christians was to look on the departed as no otherwise severed from them than the man who has gone to New York is divided from his family in Boston. He is not within the scope of the senses, he can not be addressed, but he is the same person, with the same heart, still living and loving, and partners with them of all joys and sorrows.

But while they considered personal identity and consciousness unchanged and the friend as belonging to them, as much after death as before, they regarded his death as an advancement, an honor, a glory. It was customary, we are told, to celebrate the day of his death as his birth-day—the day when he was born to new immortal life. Tertullian, who died in the year 2.0, in his treatise called the *Soldier's Chaplet*, says: "We make anniversary oblations for the dead—for their birth-days," meaning the day of their death. In another place he says, "It was the practice of a widow to pray for the soul of her deceased husband, desiring on his behalf present refreshment or rest, and a part in the first resurrection," and offering annually for him oblation on the day of his *falling asleep*. By this gentle term the rest of the body in the grave was always spoken of among Christians. It is stated that on these anniversary days of commemorating the dead they were used to make a feast, inviting both clergy and people, but especially the poor and needy, the widows and orphans, that it might not only be a memorial of rest to the dead, but a memorial of a sweet savor in the sight of God.

A Christian funeral was in every respect a standing contrast to the lugubrious and depressing gloom of modern times. Palms and olive branches were carried in the funeral procession, and the cypress was rejected as symbolizing gloom. Psalms and hymns of a joyful and triumphant tone were sung around the corpse while it was kept in the house and on the way to the grave. St. Chrysostom, speaking of funeral services, quotes passages from the psalms and hymns that were in common use, thus:

"What mean our psalms and hymns? Do we not glorify God and give him thanks that he hath crowned him that has departed, that he hath delivered him from trouble, that he hath set him free from all fear? Consider what thou singest at the time. 'Turn again to thy rest, O my soul, for the Lord hath rewarded thee;' and again: 'I will fear no evil because thou art with me;' and again: 'Thou art my refuge from the affliction that compasseth me about.' Consider what these psalms mean. If thou believest the things which thou sayest to be true, why dost thou weep and lament and make a pageantry and a mock of thy singing? If thou believest them *not* to be true, why dost thou play the hypocrite so much as to sing?"

Coleman says, also:

"The sacrament of the Lord's Supper was administered at funerals and often at the grave itself. By this rite it was professed that the communion of saints was still perpetuated between the living and the dead. It was a favorite idea that both still continued members of the same mystical body, the same on earth and in heaven."—*Antiq.*, p. 418.

Coleman says, also, that the early Christian utterly discarded all the Jewish badges and customs of mourning, such as sackcloth and ashes and rent garments, and severely censured the Roman custom of wearing black.

St. Augustine says: "Why should we disfigure ourselves with black, unless we would imitate unbelieving nations, not only in their wailing for the dead, but also in their mourning apparel? Be assured, these are foreign and unlawful usages."

He says, also: "Our brethren are not to be mourned for being liberated from this world when we know that they are not *om*itted but *pre*mitted, receding from us only that they may precede us, so that journeying and voyaging before us they are to be *desired* but not lamented. Neither should we put on black raiment for them when they have already taken their white garments; and occasion should not be given to the Gentiles that they should rightly and justly reprove us, that we grieve over those as extinct and lost who we say are now alive with God, and the faith that we profess by voice and speech we deny by the testimony of our heart and bosom."

Are not many of the usages and familiar forms of speech of modern Christendom a return to old heathenism? Are they not what St. Augustine calls a repudiation of the Christian faith? The black garments, the funeral dreariness, the mode of speech which calls a departed friend lost —have they not become the almost invariable rule in Christian life?

So really and truly did the first Christians believe that their friends were still one with themselves, that they considered them even in their advanced and glorified state a subject of prayers.

Prayer for each other was to the first Christians a reality. The intimacy of their sympathy, the entire oneness of their life, made prayer for each other a necessity, and they prayed for each other instinctively as they prayed for themselves. So, St. Paul says "*Always* in *every* prayer of mine making request for you always with joy." Christians are commanded without ceasing to pray for each other. As their faith forbade them to consider the departed as lost or ceasing to exist, or in any way being out of their fellowship and communion, it did not seem to them strange or improper to yield to that impulse of the loving heart which naturally breathes to the Heavenly Father the name of its beloved. On the contrary, it was a custom in the earliest Christian times, in the solemn service of the Eucharist, to commend to God in a memorial prayer the souls of their friends *departed*, but not *dead*. In Coleman's *Antiquities*, and other works of the same kind, many instances of this are given. We select some:

Arnobius, in his treatise against the heathen writers, probably in 305, speaking of the prayers offered after the consecration of the elements in the Lord's Supper, says "that Christians prayed for pardon and peace in behalf of the living and dead." Cyril, of Jerusalem, reports the prayer made after consecrating the elements in Holy Communion in these words :

"We offer this sacrifice in memory of those who have fallen asleep before us, first patriarchs, prophets, apostles, and martyrs, that God by their prayers and supplications may receive our supplications and those we pray for, our holy fathers and bishops, and all that have fallen asleep before us, believing it is of great advantage to their sou's to be prayed for while the holy and tremendous sacrifice lies upon the altar."

A memorial of this custom has come into the Protestant Church in the Episcopal Eucharistic service where occur these words : "And we also bless thy Holy Name for all thy servants departed this life in thy faith and fear, beseeching Thee to give us grace so to follow their good examples, that we with them may be partakers of thy Heavenly Kingdom." It will be seen here the progress of an idea, its corruption and its reform.

The original idea with the primitive Christian was this : "My friend is neither dead nor changed. He is only gone before me, and is promoted to higher joy ; but he is still mine and I am his. Still can I pray for him, still can he pray for me ; and as when he was here on earth we can be mutually helped by each other's prayers."

Out of this root—so simple and so sweet—grew idolatrous exaggerations of saint worship and a monstrous system of bargain and sale of prayers for the dead. The Reformation swept all this away—and, as usual with reformations, swept away a portion of the primitive truth—but it retained still the Eucharistic memorial of departed friends as a fragment of primitive simplicity.

The Church, furthermore, appointed three festivals of commemoration of these spiritual members of the great Church Invi-ible with whom they held fellowship—the festivals of All Souls, of All Angels, of All Saints.

Two of these are still retained in the Episcopal Church the feast of St. Michael and All Angels, and the feast of All Saints. These days are derived from those yearly anniversaries which were common in the primitive ages

[Here we have a formal deprecation of the tendency of modern orthodoxy to withdraw from what was once regarded as a proper religious belief and sentiment, and which modern Spiritualists warmly accept, and make one of the chief grounds for their doctrine of intercommunication between the departed dead and the living. We expect to give our readers other papers by Mrs. Stowe in continuation of her discussion on the subject.

In the following letter, or extract from a letter, from Mr. Andrew Jackson Davis, one of the leading lights and exponents of Spiritualism at the present day, we have a voice from the *inside*, furnishing some information with regard to the state of spiritualistic affairs in America, and some of the expected results of the movement.]

"Spiritualism, for the most part, is a *shower* from the realm of intelligences and uncultured affections. It is rapidly irrigating and fertilizing everything that has root and the seed-power to grow. It is starting up the half-dead trees of Sectarianism, causing the most miserable weeds to grow rapid and rank, and of course, attracting very general attention to religious feelings and super-terrene existences.

"As an effect of this spiritualistic rain, you may look for an immense harvest of both wheat and tares—the grandest growths in great principles and ideas on the one hand, and a fearful crop of crudities and disorganizing superstitions on the other. There will be seen floating on the flood many of our most sacred institutions. Old wagon-ruts, long-forgotten cow-tracks, every little hole and corner in the old highways, will be filled to the brim with the rain. You will hardly know the difference between the true springs and the flowing mud-pools visible on every side. Many noble minds will stumble as they undertake to ford the new streams which will come up to their very door-sills, if not into their sacred and established habitations. Perhaps lives may be lost; perhaps homes may be broken up; perhaps fortunes may be sacrificed; for who ever heard of a great flood, a storm of much power, or an earthquake, that did not do one, or two, or *all* of these deplorable things? Spiritualism is, indeed, all and everything which its worst enemies or best friends ever said of it;—a great rain from heaven, a storm of violence, a power unto salvation, a destroyer and a builder too—each, and all, and everything good, bad, and indifferent; for which every one, nevertheless, should be thankful, as eventually all will be when the evil subsides, when the severe rain is over, and the clouds dispersed—when even the blind will see with new eyes, the lame walk, and the mourners of the world be made to rejoice with joy unspeakable.

"Of course, my kind brother, you know that I look upon 'wisdom' organized into our daily lives, and 'love' inspiring every heart, as the only true heaven appointed saviour of mankind. And all spiritual growth and intellectual advancement in the goodnesses and graces of this redeemer I call an application of the Harmonial Philosophy. But I find, as most likely you do, that it is as hard to get the Spiritualists to become Harmonial Philosophers as to induce ardent Bible-believers to daily practice the grand essentials which dwell in the warm heart of Christianity."

It is not long since the writer was in conversation with a very celebrated and popular minister of the modern Church, who has for years fulfilled a fruitful ministry in New England. He was speaking of modern Spiritualism as one of the most dangerous forms of error—as an unaccountable infatuation. The idea was expressed by a person present that it was after all true that the spirits of the departed friends were in reality watching over our course and interested in our affairs in this world.

The clergyman, who has a fair right, by reason of his standing and influence to represent the New England pulpit, met that idea by a prompt denial. "A pleasing sentimental dream," he said, "very apt to mislead, and for which there is no scriptural and rational foundation." We have shown in our last article what the very earliest Christians were in the habit of thinking with regard to the unbroken sympathy between the living and those called dead, and how the Church by very significant and solemn acts pronounced them to be not only alive, but alive in a fuller, higher, and more joyful sense than those on earth.

We may remember that among the primitive Christians the celebration of the Lord's Supper was not as in our modern times a rare and unfrequent occurence, coming at intervals of two, three, and even six months, but that it occured every Sunday, and on many of the solemn events of life, as funerals and marriages, and that one part of the celebration always consisted in recognizing by a solemn prayer the unbroken unity of the saints below and the saints in heaven. We may remember, too, that it was a belief among them that angels were invisibly present, witnessing and uniting with the eucharistic memorial—a belief of which we still have the expression in that solemn portion of the Episcopal communion service which says, "Wherefore with angels and archangels, and with all the company of heaven, we laud and magnify thy Holy Name."

This part of the eucharistic service was held by the first Christians to be the sacred and mysterious point of confluence when the souls of saints on earth and the blessed in heaven united. So says Saint Chrysostom:

"The seraphim above sing the holy Trisagion hymn; the holy congregation of men on earth send up the same; the general assembly of celestial and earthly creatures join together; there is one thanksgiving, one exultation; one choir of men and angels rejoicing together."

And in another place he says:

"The martyrs are now rejoicing in concert, partaking of the mystical songs of the heavenly choir. For if while they were in the body whenever they communicated in the sacred mysteries they made part of the choir, singing with the cherubim, 'holy, holy, holy,' as ye all that are initiated in the holy mysteries know; much more now, being joined with those whose partners they were in the earthly choir, they do with greater freedom partake of those solemn glorifications of God above."

The continued identity, interest and unbroken oneness of the departed with the remaining was a topic frequently insisted on among early Chiistian ministers—it was one reason of the rapid spread of Christianity. Converts flocked in clouds to the ranks of a people who professed to have vanquished death—in whose inclosure love was forever safe, and who by so many sacred and solemn acts of recognition consoled the bereaved heart with this thought, that their beloved, though unseen, was still living and loving—still watching, waiting, and caring for them.

Modern rationalistic religion says: "We do not know anything about them—God has taken them: of them and their estate we know nothing: whether they remember us, whether they know what we are doing, whether they care for us, whether we shall ever see them again to know them, are all questions vailed in inscrutable mystery. We must give our friends up wholly and take refuge in God."

But St. Augustine, speaking on the same subject, says:

"Therefore, if we wish to hold communion with the saints in eternal life we must think much of imitating them. They ought to recognize in us something of their virtues, that they may better offer their supplications to God for us. These [virtues] are the foot-prints which the blessed returning to their country have left, that we shall follow their path to joy. Why should we not hasten and run after them that we too may see our fatherland? There a great crowd of dear ones are awaiting us, of parents, brethren, children, a multitudinous host are longing for us—now secure of their own safety, and anxious only for our salvation."

Now let us take the case of some poor, widowed mother, from whose heart has been torn an only son—pious, brave, and beautiful—her friend, her pride, her earthly hope—struck down suddenly as by a lightning stroke. The physical shock is terrible—the cessation of communion, if the habits of intercourse and care, if the habit, so sweet to the Christian, of praying for that son, must all cease. We can see now what the primitive Church would have said to such a mother: "Thy son is *not* dead. To the Christian there is no death—follow his footsteps, imitate his prayerfulness and watchfulness, and that he may the better pray for thee, keep close in the great communion of saints." Every Sabbath would bring to her the eucharistic feast, when the Church on earth and the Church in heaven held their reunion, where " with angels and archangels, and all the company of heaven," they join their praises ! and she might feel herself drawing near to her blessed one in glory. How consoling—how comforting such Church fellowship !

A mother under such circumstances would feel no temptation to resort to doubtful, perplexing sources, to glean here and there fragments of that consolation which the Church was ordained to give. In every act of life the primitive Church recognized that the doors of heaven were open through her ordinances and the communion of love with the departed blest unbroken.

It has been our lot to know the secret history of many who are not outwardly or professedly Spiritualists — persons of sober and serious habits of thought, of great self-culture and self-restraint, to whom it happened after the death of a friend to meet accidentally and without any seeking or expecting on their part with spiritualistic phenomena of a very marked type. These are histories that never will be unvailed to the judgment of a scoffing and unsympathetic world ; that in the very na ture of the case must forever remain secret; yet they have brought to hearts bereaved and mourning that very consolation which the Christian Church ought to have afforded them, and which the primitive Church so amply provided.

In conversation with such, we have often listened to remarks like this: "I do not seek these things—I do not search out mediums nor attend spiritual circles. I have attained all I wish to know, and am quite indifferent now whether I see another manifestation." "And what," we inquired, "is this something that you have attained?" "Oh, I feel perfectly certain that my friend is not dead—but alive, unchanged, in a region of joy and blessedness, expecting me, and praying for me, and often ministering to me."

Compare this with the language of St. Augustine, and we shall see that it is simply a return to the stand-point of the primitive Church.

Among the open and professed Spiritualists are some men and women of pure and earnest natures, and seriously anxious to do good, and who ought to be distinguished from the charlatans who have gone into it merely from motives of profit and self-interest. Now it is to be remarked that this higher class of spiritualists, with one voice, declare that the subject of spiritual communication is embarrassed with formidable difficulties. They admit that lying spirits often frequent the circle, that they are powerful to deceive, and that the means of distinguishing between the wiles of evil spirits and the communications of good ones are very obscure.

This, then, is the prospect. The pastures of the Church have been suffered to become bare and barren of one species of food which the sheep crave and sicken for the want of. They break out of the inclosure and rush, unguided, searching for it among poisonous plants, which closely resemble it, but whose taste is deadly.

Those remarkable phenomena which affect belief upon this subject are not confined to paid mediums and spiritual circles, so called. They sometimes come of themselves to persons neither believing in them, looking for them, nor seeking them. Thus coming they can not but powerfully and tenderly move the soul. A person in the desolation of bereavement, visited with such experiences, is in a condition which calls for the tenderest sympathy and most careful guidance. Yet how little of this is there to be found! The attempt to unvail their history draws upon them, perhaps, only cold ridicule and a scarcely suppressed doubt of their veracity. They are repelled from making confidence where they ought to find the wisest guidance, and are drawn by an invisible sympathy into labyrinths of deception and error—and finally, perhaps, relapse into a colder skepticism than before. That such experiences are becoming common in our days, is a fact that ought to rouse true Christians to consideration, and to searching the word of God to find the real boundaries and the true and safe paths.

We have stated in the last article, and in this, what the belief and the customs of the primitive Christians were in respect to the departed. We are aware that it does not follow, of course, that a custom is to be adopted in our times because the first Christians preached and taught it. A man does not become like his ancestors by dressing up in their old clothes—but by acting in their *spirit*. It is quite possible to wear such robes and practice such ceremonies as the early Christians did and not to be in the least like them. Therefore let us not be held as advocating the practice of administering the eucharist at funerals, and of praying for the dead in the eucharistic service, because it was done in the first three centuries. But we do hold to a return to the *spirit* which caused these customs. We hold to *that belief* in the unbroken unity possible between those who have passed to the higher life than this. We hold to that vivid faith in things unseen which was the strength of primitive Christians. The first Christians *believed* what they said they did—we do not. The unseen spiritual world, its angels and archangels, its saints and martyrs, its purity and its joys, were ever before them, and that is why they were such a mighty force in the world. St. Augustine says that it was the vision of the saints gone before that inspired them with courage and contempt of death—and it is true.

In another paper we shall endeavor to show how far these beliefs of the primitive Church correspond with the Holy Scripture,

DR. DODDRIDGE'S DREAM

[In concluding these Psychological discussions, what is there more appropriate than the following? If it be called only a dream, or, even a delusion, what harm can come of it? Is it not in keeping with Scripture teachings, as now interpreted? For ourselves, we enjoy our own opinions on subjects not susceptible of proof to the external senses. Others may do the same. EDITOR.]

DR. DODDRIDGE was on terms of very intimate friendship with Dr. Samuel Clarke, and in religious conversation they spent many happy hours together. Among other matters, a very favorite topic was the intermediate state of the soul, and the probability that at the instant of dissolution it was introduced into the presence of all the heavenly hosts, and the splendors around the throne of God. One evening, after a conversation of this nature, Dr. Doddridge retired to rest, and "in the visions of the night" his ideas were shaped into the following beautiful form.

He dreamed that he was at the house of a friend, when he was taken suddenly and dangerously ill. By degrees he seemed to grow worse, and at last to expire. In an instant he was sensible that he had exchanged the prison-house and sufferings of mortality for a state of liberty and happiness. Embodied in a slender, aerial form, he seemed to float in a region of pure light. Beneath him lay the earth, but not a glittering city or a village, the forest or the sea were visible. There was naught to be seen below save the melancholy group of his friends, weeping around his lifeless remains. Himself thrilled with delight, he was surprised at their tears, and attempted to inform them of his happy change, but by some mysterious power, utterance was denied; and as he anxiously leaned over the mourning circle, gazing fondly upon them and struggling to speak, he rose silently upon the air, their forms became more and more indistinct, and gradually melted away from his sight. Reposing upon golden clouds, he found himself swiftly mounting the skies, with a venerable figure at his side, guiding his mysterious movements, and in whose countenance he discovered the lineaments of youth and age blended together, with an intimate harmony and majestic sweetness.

They traveled together through a vast region of empty space, until, at length, the battlements of a glorious edifice shone in the distance, and as its form rose brilliant and distinct among the far-off shadows that flitted athwart their path, the guide informed him that the palace he beheld was, for the present, to be his mansion of rest. Gazing upon its splendor, he replied that while on earth he had often heard that eye had not seen, nor ear heard, nor could the heart of man conceive, the things which God hath prepared for those who love him; but notwithstanding the building to which they were rapidly approaching was superior to anything he had before beheld, yet its grandeur had not exceeded the conceptions he had formed. The guide made no reply—they were already at the door, and entered. The guide introduced him into a spacious apartment, at the extremity of which stood a table, covered with a snow-white cloth, a golden cup, and a cluster of grapes, and then said that he must leave him, but that *he* must remain, for in a short time he would receive a visit from the lord of the mansion, and that during the interval before his arrival, the apartment would furnish him sufficient entertainment and instruction. The guide vanished, and he was left alone. He began to examine the decorations of the room, and observed that the walls were adorned with a number of pictures. Upon nearer inspection he perceived, to his astonishment, that they formed a complete biography of his own life. Here he saw depicted, that angels, though unseen, had ever been his familiar attendants; and sent by God they had sometimes preserved him from imminent peril. He beheld himself first represented as an infant just expiring, when his life was prolonged by an angel gently breathing into his nostrils. Most of the occurrences delineated were perfectly familiar to his recollection, and unfolded many things which he had never before understood, and which had perplexed him with many doubts and much uneasiness. Among others he was particularly impressed with a picture in which he was represented as falling from his horse, when death would have been inevitable had not an angel received him in his arms and broken the force of his descent. These merciful interpositions of God filled him with joy and gratitude, and his heart overflowed with love as he surveyed in them all an exhibition of goodness and mercy far beyond all that he had imagined.

Suddenly his attention was arrested by a knock at the door. The lord of the mansion had arrived—the door opened and he entered. So powerful and overwhelming, and withal of such singular beauty was his appearance, that he sank down at his feet, completely overcome by his majestic presence. His lord gently raised him from the ground, and taking his hand led him forward to the table. He pressed with his fingers the juice of the grapes into the golden cup, and after having himself drank, he presented it to him, saying, "This is the new wine in my Father's kingdom." No sooner had he partaken than all uneasy sensations vanished, perfect love had now cast out fear, and he conversed with the Saviour as an intimate friend. Like the silver rippling of a summer sea he heard fall from his lips the grateful approbation: "Thy labors are finished, thy work is approved; rich and glorious is the reward." Thrilled with an unspeakable bliss, that pervaded the very depths of his soul, he suddenly saw glories upon glories bursting upon his view. The Doctor awoke. Tears of rapture from this joyful interview were rolling down his cheeks. Long did the lively impression of this charming dream remain upon his mind, and never could he speak of it without emotions of joy, and with tender and grateful remembrance.

BRAIN and MIND;
OR,
MENTAL SCIENCE CONSIDERED IN ACCORDANCE WITH THE PRINCIPLES OF PHRENOLOGY,
AND
IN RELATION TO MODERN PHYSIOLOGY.

By HENRY S. DRAYTON, A.M., M.D., and JAMES McNEILL, A.B. Illustrated with over 100 Portraits and Diagrams. 12mo, extra cloth, $1.50.

This contribution to the science of mind has been made in response to the demand of the time for a work embodying the grand principles of Phrenology, as they are understood and applied to-day by the advanced exponents of mental philosophy, who accept the doctrine taught by Gall, Spurzheim, and Combe.

The following, from the Table of Contents, shows the scope of the work:

General Principles; Of the Temperaments; Structure of the Brain and Skull; Classification of the Faculties; The Selfish Organs; The Intellect; The Semi-Intellectual Faculties; The Organs of the Social Functions; The Selfish Sentiments; The Moral and Religious Sentiments; How to Examine Heads; How Character is Manifested; The Action of the Faculties; The Relation of Phrenology to Metaphysics and Education; Value of Phrenology as an Art; Phrenology and Physiology; Objections and Confirmations by the Physiologists; Phrenology in General Literature.

NOTICES OF THE PRESS.

"Phrenology is no longer a thing laughed at. The scientific researches of the last twenty years have demonstrated the fearful and wonderful complication of matter, not only with mind, but with what we call moral qualities. Thereby, we believe, the divine origin of 'our frame' has been newly illustrated, and the Scriptural psychology confirmed; and in the Phrenological Chart we are disposed to find a species of 'urim and thummim,' revealing, if not the Creator's will concerning us, at least His revelation of essential character. The above work is, without doubt, the best popular presentation of the science which has yet been made. It confines itself strictly to facts, and is not written in the interest of any pet 'theory.' It is made very interesting by its copious illustrations, pictorial and narrative, and the whole is brought down to the latest information on this curious and suggestive department of knowledge."—*Christian Intelligencer, N. Y.*

"Whether a reader be inclined to believe Phrenology or not, he must find the volume a mine of interest, gather many suggestions of the highest value, and rise from its perusal with clearer views of the nature of mind and the responsibilities of human life. The work constitutes a complete text-book on the subject."—*Presbyterian Journal, Philadelphia.*

"In 'Brain and Mind' the reader will find the fundamental ideas on which Phrenology rests fully set forth and analyzed, and the science clearly and practically treated. It is not at all necessary for the reader to be a believer in the science to enjoy the study of the latest exposition of its methods. The literature of the science is extensive, but so far as we know there is no one book which so comprehensively as 'Brain and Mind' defines its limits and treats of its principles so thoroughly, not alone philosophically, but also in their practical relation to the everyday life of man."—*Cal. Advertiser.*

In style and treatment it is adapted to the general reader, abounds with valuable instruction expressed in clear, practical terms, and the work constitutes by far the best Text-book on Phrenology published, and is adapted to both private and class study.

The illustrations of the Special Organs and Faculties are for the most part from portraits of men and women whose characters are known, and great pains have been taken to exemplify with accuracy the significance of the text in each case. For the student of mind and character the work is of the highest value. By mail, post paid, on receipt of price, $1.50. Address,

FOWLER & WELLS CO., Publishers, 753 Broadway, N. Y.

6. Combativeness.   3. Friendship.

THE PHRENOLOGICAL JOURNAL

is widely known in America and Europe, having been before the reading world fifty years, and occupying a place in literature exclusively its own, viz.: the study of **Human Nature.**

It has long met with the approval of the press and the people, and as a means of introducing the JOURNAL and extending an interest in the subject, we have prepared a new **Phrenological Chart.** This is a handsome lithograph of a symbolical head, in which the relative location of each of the organs is shown by special designs illustrating the function of each in the human mind.

These sketches are not simply outlines, as shown above, but many of them are little gems of artistic design and coloring in themselves, and will help the student to locate the faculties and to impress his mind with a correct idea of their prime functions.

For instance, **Combativeness** is represented by a scene in a lawyer's office, where a disagreement has led to an angry dispute; **Secretiveness** is shown by a picture of the cunning fox attempting to visit a hen-roost by the light of the moon; the teller's desk in a bank represents **Acquisitiveness;** a butcher's shop is made to stand for **Destructiveness;** the familiar scene of the "Good Samaritan" exhibits the influence of **Benevolence; Sublimity** is pictured by a sketch of the grand scenery of the Yosemite Valley.

The Chart also contains a printed Key, giving the names and definitions of the different faculties. The whole picture is very ornamental, and must prove a feature of peculiar attraction wherever it is seen; nothing like it for design and finish being elsewhere procurable.

It is mounted with rings for hanging on the wall, and will be appropriate for the home, office, library, or school. The head itself is about twelve inches wide, beautifully lithographed in colors, on heavy plate paper, about 19 x 24 inches. Price, $1.00. It is published and offered as a special premium for subscribers to the **Phrenological Journal** for 1885. To those who prefer it, we will send the Phrenological Bust as a premium. The Journal is published at $2.00 a year, with 15 cents extra required when the Chart or Bust is sent. Single Number, 20 cents. Address

FOWLER & WELLS CO., Publishers, 753 Broadway, N. Y.

www.ingramcontent.com/pod-product-compliance
Lightning Source LLC
Chambersburg PA
CBHW020121170426
43199CB00009B/579